MAKING CHANGES

MAKING CHANGES

A PRACTICAL GUIDE TO VERNACULAR HARMONY

BY ERIC SALZMAN
AND MICHAEL SAHL

McGraw-Hill Book Company
New York   St. Louis   San Francisco   London
Düsseldorf   Mexico   Toronto   Sydney

This book is dedicated to all those musicians who, in making their changes, created this harmony. Some of their names appear in this book but most are, of necessity, unmentioned; we are grateful nonetheless.

There are a few people who must be thanked by name:

Charles Komanoff for his ability to think of songs that actually use these changes; many of the Tunes To Listen To (TTLTs) were supplied by him.

Stuart Isacoff and Charles Komanoff for giving us feedback on our unconventional approach, the one from the professional point of view, the other from that of the educated amateur.

Joseph Taubman for helping us with the mysteries of copyright.

Steven Dydo who copied all the music in the book and thereby rendered the illegible legible (not to say beautiful).

Iris Weinstein who performed the impossible task of making this book look the way we wanted it to and making it look her way (i.e. good) at the same time.

Veronica Windholz for making everything happen and keeping everybody talking to everybody else.

Joyce Johnson for the editorial courage and fortitude to support and see through—with very few guidelines or precedents—a difficult and unconventional project.

Library of Congress Cataloging in Publication Data

Salzman, Eric.
    Making changes.

    1. Harmony, Keyboard. 2. Music, Popular (Songs, etc.)—Instruction and study. I. Sahl, Michael, 1934–   joint author. II. Title.
MT224.S155M3   781.3   76-25201
ISBN 0-07-054489-1
ISBN 0-07-054488-3 pbk.

123456789BA BA7987

CONTENTS

INTRODUCTION

Students and musicians who want to learn something about harmony can find learned treatises and classical texts that, at their best, help prepare them for a gig in a provincial German town, circa 1760. Along with this useful knowledge comes a great deal of guilt, snobbery, and abuse.

What is almost impossible to find is useful knowledge about the harmony—the changes—that musicians actually use, as opposed to what European musicians used two hundred years ago.

The problem is that the European tradition is both respectable and dead and, therefore, suitable for pedagogy. The American tradition—the living one—is hand-me-down dialect, originally spoken by people of no social standing whatever.

Since about 1830, the music teachers of America have felt it their sacred mission to improve the manners of their countrymen—to teach them to use the right musical fork: get rid of parallel fifths, keep consistent voice-leading, eliminate cross relations, not skip to dissonances, prepare smooth modulations, and so forth.

Fortunately these efforts have been largely in vain, and a rich body of common harmonic practice has arisen, quite as distinctive as the melody and rhythm that go with it. This common practice—which, after Wiley Hitchcock, we like to call "vernacular harmony"—is a living language. Until now it has been learned largely by imitation and memorization. This is a workable way of transmitting traditional knowledge as long as the cultural tradition remains tight. But, for better or for worse, we are living in an age when all the various popular styles seem to coexist at once in a kind of grand common practice, and this is true even in the most obscure boondocks. Instead of a single, simple mainstream tradition, there is a kind of historical and cross-cultural interweave. We have a tremendous amount of accumulated knowledge and no easy way to get an essential grasp of it.

Although American popular, or vernacular, harmony is a compound of many different elements—black, white, city, country—there are, in fact, many underlying unities. These things can be learned. They don't tell the whole story, but we believe they tell something useful and important about our culture.

The kind of vernacular harmony discussed in this book is largely of the Americas (Latin as well as North), although its origins can be traced to many parts of the world. Of course it is no longer purely American, but has become common in many parts of the world in a variety of cultural and political guises.

Harmony, in its origins, is a European invention. In American common practice it has been vastly altered by modal melody and harmony, from Anglo-Saxon and Celtic folk and West African sources, and by rhythmic practice, largely Afro-American in origin.

European tonal harmony reached these shores in various forms: the old hymns, the semi-popular European classics, the popular song and dance music of the nineteenth century. It is a strong element in the traditional forms of gospel, ragtime, blues, standard pop, country music, and much jazz. But this harmony did not remain unchanged. It had to accommodate itself to melodies that grew up without any harmony. It had to remain within certain kinds of phrase structures even if the chords went "far out." Major developments took place on the piano and the guitar where there was no consistency in the number of parts as there would be in a string quartet, an orchestra, or a choir. Chords came to be modular building blocks, connected to each other by function and not by the movement of the parts.

Another important difference between European tonal harmony and its vernacular descendants has to do with the sense of key. European music after 1700 is always in movement away from or back to the central key. In vernacular harmony, until very recently, the sense of the home key is crucial; even a "weird bridge" comes back very quickly to the key. All of the harmonic changes, no matter how far-out, can be heard against and colored by reference to the tonic in the same way that the rhythmic sophistications of traditional jazz are measured against and made comprehensible by the beat.

Modal melody has long been a factor in the evolution of vernacular harmony. Modal melody cannot be harmonized effectively without stretching or altering the meaning or changing the chords of traditional harmony. There is also a phenomenon that we can call modal harmony, including many kinds of changes that do not occur in traditional or tonal harmony. The origins of modal harmony are obscure; it appears in folk harmony before the twentieth century, but its great vogue and development comes in the twentieth century through symphonic and commercial music, as well as the arrangements and popularizations of folk material. This harmonic style has had a flowering in recent years with the folk, rock, and modal jazz movements.

It is worth pointing out that modern classical tonal music which is not primarily based on voice-leading principles—Debussy, Ravel, Stravinsky, Milhaud, Copland, various national styles, and even some more recent music—has much in common with popular practice. Many kinds of cross-fertilization have taken place over the entire course of the century.

A wide vocabulary of chords and usages has developed out of these intermixtures and hybridizations. A modal melody, which may include "out-of-tune" or "blue" notes may be harmonized with modal chords, foreign to classical tradition, or the most classical of progressions "incorrectly" voiced, or some combination of the two. The basic elements of the simpler styles may be developed with added notes and richer sonorities, which obey no rules except those of the ear. It is senseless to "correct" these practices—it has been tried without success. What we want is to understand them, appreciate them for their continuing vitality and communicative values, and use them as stepping stones to saying something new within a common practice—the oldest and perhaps still the truest path for creativity.

A chord in the hand is worth two in the book.
A. Bell

HOW TO USE THIS BOOK

This book is really meant to be used at the piano. It can be used with the guitar, but you have to be able to find your way around the guitar. You have to be able to read music—even the bass clef—but no other advance preparation is required.

The heart of the book is in the musical examples. If you were to play through the examples and never read a word of the text, you would learn most of what we have to tell. The text is conceived as a commentary on the music and an aid to understanding it. It is not really necessary to start from the beginning and work on through, but there is some sequence to the treatment and some progression of easy to hard, old to new, simple to complex.

The chords in most of the examples are not "real," finished music, but rather the harmonic understructure. These progressions should be played slowly and with a feeling of time: say a bar of medium time for each note.

A lot of these examples only make sense if you listen to the kind of "real" music from which they are derived. We have sometimes expanded our treatment to give chord backgrounds or full-fledged notations of "real" music—quoted or made up. In these expanded treatments we get into styles. We have also given the names of pieces of music that use these changes: **TTLT** means "Tunes To Listen To."

Popular music is usually thought of as a series of styles. We have not organized the book this way but, nevertheless, there is a great deal of material in the styles of famous performers, bands, or arrangers. This is fun for everyone and helps the book. What you should be able to do is to recognize chords, to put them together in progressions (or "changes"), and to substitute new ones in place of old ones. This is not the same thing as composing, but it is an absolutely essential tool for writing music with anything more than the three basic chords.

Not every chord that has ever been struck is here (although a very large percentage of them are), but if you can familiarize yourself with what goes on in this book, new chords will hold no terrors.

This book does not really proceed in the manner of a textbook, "from the simple to the complex." We were never able to decide what was the most simple and what the most complex. Also, many of the most familiar sounds in people's ears are "complex" in the sense that they are made of leftovers of more than one structure. So, instead, this book is like a walk in the woods. If you go on a walk with someone who knows about the woods, they will tell you sometimes the common name for something, sometimes the scientific name. This may be the first time you have ever seen a Trillium or a Brown Thrasher, but, since things tend to be found over again on the same walk, pretty soon you begin to catch on and remember things. Eventually, you begin to understand the logic of the scientific names and families and even the relationship between the living things in the forest. Interest and recognition produce knowledge rather than the other way around, and each new acquisition, each new walk in the woods, each new understanding makes the one after still easier.

Note to Non–Piano Players:

The piano is a music machine that anyone can learn to operate—at least enough to play the basic changes. If the first section of the book ("Blues Changes") is too difficult, skip to the following sections. Most of the examples in this book are simple changes which anyone can play. Trying them out at a piano is in itself a way of learning some keyboard. The written-out arrangements are more difficult, but they also serve as a basic introduction to piano styles.

Note on Guitar Chords:

Chord names are indicated by Roman numerals. All seventh, ninth, eleventh, and thirteenth chords are major unless otherwise indicated. Small *m* preceding a chord means *minor*, *sus* means *suspended*, *dim* means *diminished*, *aug* means *augmented*, and *add* means *add the tone* (I add6). 7–5 is the same as a dominant seventh except that the fifth is lowered (diminished). 7+5 is the same as the dominant seventh except that the fifth is raised (augmented). *S/S/* means *slide*. A large slash (as in IV/V or G/F♯) indicates a chord over a different bass note.

Note on Notation:

When we give changes with rhythm or bars (usually written in whole notes), sharps and flats apply only to the notes they precede. When there are bar-lines, sharps and flats hold through the measures as usual.

Note on Musical Examples:

Unfortunately, permission to quote from a few standard tunes was not obtainable. For these, you will have to refer to your own sheet music.

MAKING CHANGES 1: BLUES AND MODAL HARMONY CHANGES

American vernacular harmony is a mingling of two traditions. Tonal harmony came from Europe via the church, the theater, the school, and the parlor piano. It is the basic harmonic resource for barber shop, ragtime, musical comedy, gospel, popular song, jazz, early rock-and-roll, and the blues. Modal harmony comes from folk music (white and black), and it has had a very active life in country places. It spread to the cities via recordings in the Twenties and Thirties. It is a basic harmonic resource that has been used by modern composers, by the urban folk movement, and eventually in rock and recent jazz.

One way to get an idea of the possibilities of these two kinds of harmony is to take a typical melody for each and try to set it in as many different ways as possible. This is also a way to approach theory through music rather than the other way around. Much of the material of the book is here in condensed musical form. In effect, the rest of the book is devoted to showing "how it's done."

First you went to Fred Neil and learned to play Blues in E and then you went to Dave Von Ronk and learned to play Blues in C and then you got your Martin D-12 and then you were a folk singer.
John Sebastian

Blues Changes

12-bar blues; three 4-bar phrases.

Sahl/Salzman

The blues is a traditional form of Afro-American origin in which a modal melody has been harmonized with Western tonal chords.

In its original, "down-home" variety—country blues—there are many twists of melody and rhythm that are difficult or impossible to write down in conventional notation. There is often no harmony or only a single chord.

Here is an original blues in the traditional mode: 12-bar blues in three 4-bar phrases.

1-chord country blues.

Sahl/Salzman

This is the kind of embellished version of a basic melody that you might hear on a country blues record. It uses a single C[7] chord all the way through the manner of a bottleneck guitar. The rhythmic feeling is in 2 (2 beats to a bar).

Country blues with the three basic chords—I-IV-V.

Sahl/Salzman

This is the
TURNAROUND, a chord
(or group of chords) that
reintroduces the
beginning of the tune
without adding extra
bars.

This style has never really gone out of fashion. One of its great exponents, Jimmy Yancey, was active in the 1930s.

Shuffle is the rhythmic style of playing this music. It really cannot be accurately written down. In this example we wrote it like this ♪.♪.

In faster music it gets more like this ♪³♪,

and eventually like this ♪♪.

Country blues in guitar style with a few more harmonic wrinkles.

Sahl/Salzman

IV⁷ takes you back to I.

Each phrase begins with a different chord (I-IV-V⁷).

A more elaborate, urbanized harmonization with more movement in the bass and more chords.

Sahl/Salzman

IV over V or V^{11} is the chord that goes to C, but a real V^{7} is saved for the turnaround.

⌐SLIDE CHORD¬

This chord goes down to G and is a great tool of blues changes.

Stride-piano blues in the manner of Jelly Roll Morton.

Sahl/Salzman

The bass line is like a counter-melody in the first 2 phrases with an F#-dim. chord—like a slide chord that moves up instead of down.

The last phrase is a kind of harmonic payoff: a chain of dominant sevenths that is telescoped in the turnaround.

Blues for band.

Blues of this kind are associated with Bessie Smith. The bass begins to walk and the rhythmic feeling goes back and forth between 4 and 2.

The slide chord on A♭ is used to make every cadence. There are other slide chords: a diminished seventh on F# that goes up and another one on E♭ that goes down.

In the last example we had C–A⁷–D⁷–G⁷.

This time the progression is C–A⁷–A♭⁷–G⁷ (or F/G).

24

Warning: As the harmony gets more complicated, not all of the passing notes and chords show up in the guitar chords. Read the notes.

Sahl/Salzman

This is a piano version of a band arrangement with a walking bass. The music is definitely in 4 and the bass has to keep walking (whether or not he has any place to go).
The harmonies are similar to the stride-piano version, but the time feeling is different and the inner parts move with the bass in thirds (or tenths), creating a feeling of harmonic movement.

Notice that the turnaround uses both a D chord and an A-flat chord between A^7 and G^7.

1930s piano "comping" (accompanying) style with melody melting into the chords.

Sahl/Salzman

We had this dim. 7th slide progression before with F#-G in the bass.

From now on we are in 4. "Passing harmonic" sounds now have the status of full, on-the-beat chords. These chords are mostly familiar, but they don't always go where you expect them to go. Nevertheless, the principle of the slide chord is still essential. In effect, the last four bars are a series of slide chords: D9–Db9–C–Eb7–Dm7–Db9

1940s big band, Basie-style, with a walking chromatic bass.

Sahl/Salzman

The slide on A♭ is like a dom. 7th of D♭ that slides to I.

If you look at the guitar chords everything looks familiar, but if you read the notes you will find a lot going on—mostly chromatic slipping and sliding.

Notice the double slides: slide to slide (bars 7-8); slide as V of slide (bars 11-12).

1950s be-bop blues.

Sahl/Salzman

The chords are mostly major and minor sevenths which slide downward by step. These kinds of progressions are an extension of the slide chord idea, but the strong tonal feeling of earlier blues is weakened.

Contemporary modal jazz.

Sahl/Salzman

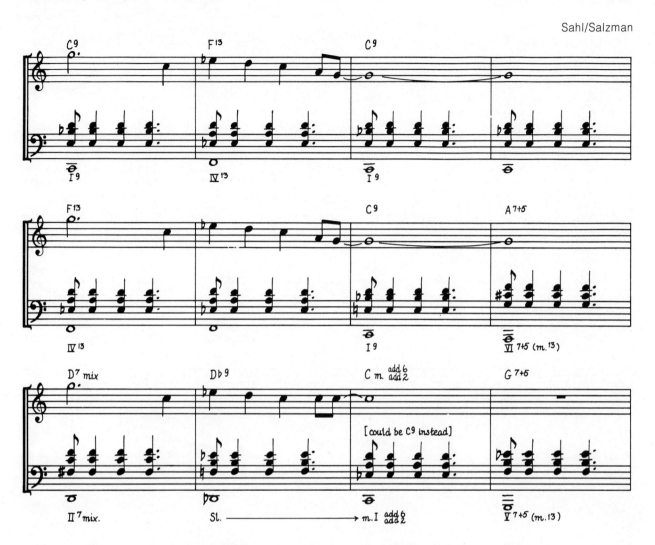

Complex chords but the underlying progression is simple, with substitutions for the old IV–V–I. Loading sevenths, ninths, etc., on a chord has the effect of restricting the number of different places to which you can move.

Modal Changes

"House Carpenter" is a traditional Anglo-American tune: four
4-bar phrases in a modal G. The original version is unaccompanied; we give a banjo accompaniment built on a modal
pattern, with no real changes.

"House Carpenter"

Traditional
All arrangements by Michael Sahl and Eric Salzman

Three modal harmonizations of "House Carpenter" using 2-note chords.

Arr. Sahl/Salzman

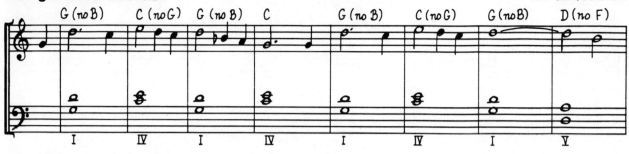

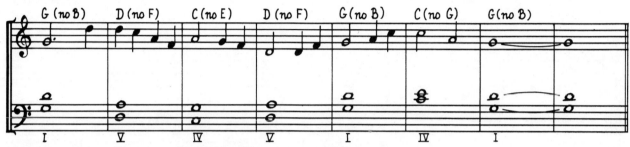

In tonal music, the return to the tonic is accomplished mostly through the dominant or dominant seventh: V–I or V⁷–I. The modal feeling of "House Carpenter" is reinforced by emphasizing IV and by eliminating the middle notes of V and I.

Arr. Sahl/Salzman

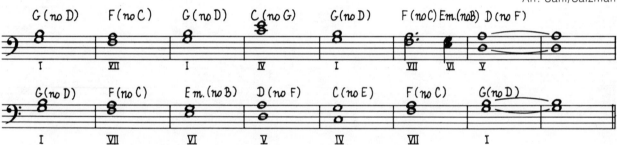

The chord on the flat seventh—F major in this case—is a strong modal sound that is almost never used in tonal harmonization. It replaces IV (C major) as a lead-in to (or lead-out from) I. VI (E minor) is another strong modal chord that forms part of a step-wise progression: I–VII–VI–V–IV. The final cadence is IV–VII–I.

Arr. Sahl/Salzman

Another modal harmonization using 2-note chords. This one uses minor V (with D and an F♮), flat III (B♭–F), and II as part of a step-wise progression: mV–IV–♭III–II–I. The cadence is IV–VII–I again.

The same tune harmonized with the basic I–IV–V–I.
[For guitar or piano]

Arr. Sahl/Salzman

Two rock arrangements.

Try singing and playing these arrangements.

Arr. Sahl/Salzman

In modal music, performance style is as important as the bare harmonic progressions. Here is a harmonization similar to the preceding, arranged in a folk or folk-rock style.

Major V—D major—is the arrival point of the first half of the tune, but the final cadence is still IV–VII–I.

Note that an arrangement may use notes that are not in the basic chords. The added notes here are part of the country style of playing.

Arr. Sahl/Salzman

Another folk-rock version with a mixture of modal tonal elements. This has strong tonal bass movement with a balance between steps and skips. The modal qualities are emphasized by the fact that IV is the lead-in chord (V—D major—is a secondary chord) and by the use of minor chords (VI–III–II) and chords on the flat side (VII, ♭III).

Two skeleton arrangements.

These harmonies would be filled out in real music (as we showed before).

Modal harmonizations tend to be freer than tonal ones, and the movement of the chords sometimes has a life of its own. The in-between harmonies—the ones that do not occur on the principal bars or accents of the melody—can be dissonant if they are reached by steps from the main harmonies.

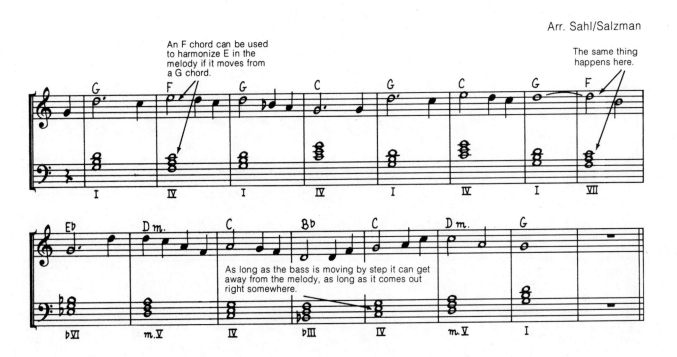

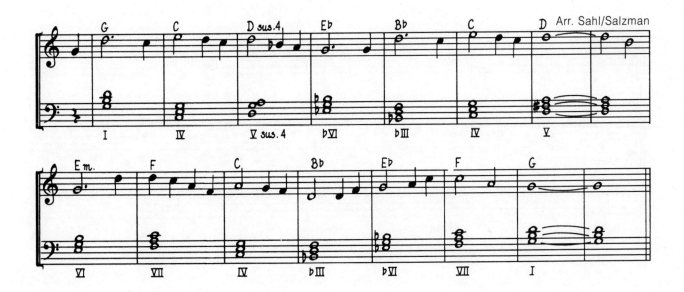

So far we have only used triads. More complex chords are
possible. Starting with this progression . . .

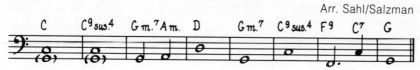

you might end up with this.

36

Or this.

Arr. Sahl/Salzman

This is on the borderline between a folk arrangement and modern classical style.

Modern rock harmonization with sevenths.

Arr. Sahl/Salzman

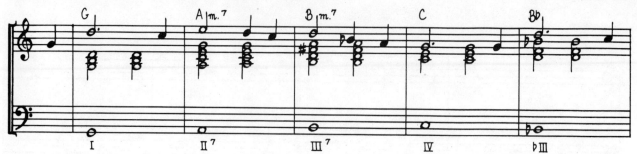

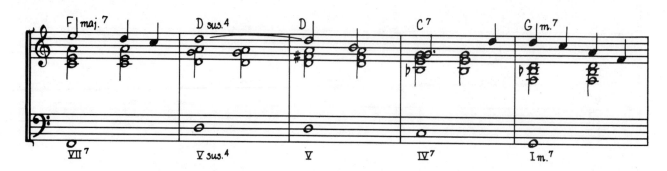

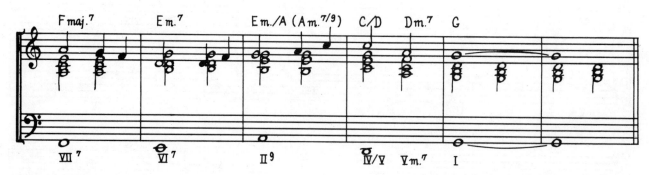

Closer to modern classical style.

Arr. Sahl/Salzman

These kinds of changes are familiar but not easy to explain. Basically, they are recombinations of standard chords and basses.

A modal jazz interpretation.

Arr. Sahl/Salzman

Again, the elements are familiar (I–VII: ♭III–IV), but the uses new. The harmony is symmetrical, static, and concentrated very much like our final blues example.

BASICS

There is no way to avoid learning the essentials. Be sure you know this material before moving ahead too quickly.

Intervals—the distances between notes—are the basic units of music. Intervals can be measured horizontally (melodically) or vertically (harmonically).

In the standard Western tuning system (twelve evenly spaced notes to the octave), the intervals look like this.

These can be played or sung melodically or as harmony.

Try singing these intervals as well as playing them.

We could start on any note, but we're starting on C.

Larger than the octave.

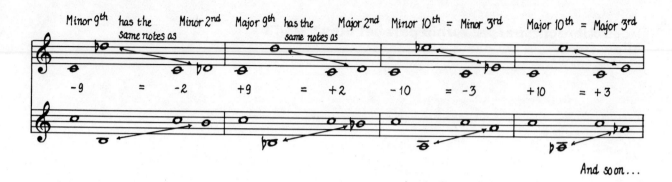

Sometimes, for various reasons, some of these intervals are written in different ways.

Here is the beginning of "House Carpenter" with the intervals labeled.

Here are the intervals counted up in C-major chord.

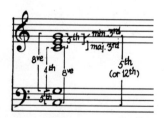

Find these intervals by playing them.

Here is the breakdown of a C dominant seventh chord, taking each of the four notes of the chord and measuring the intervals against it.

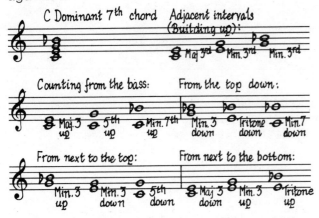

The intervals inside of chords are most often counted up from the bass, but it is important to know how to count up the intervals between the other notes as well in order to understand fully how chords work.

Scales And Modes

Musical scales are consecutive arrangements of groups of tones which constitute basic material—the tonal palette or mode of the music. Scales are alphabets for melody and harmony.

Much of the music we will be dealing with uses one or more of these basic scales or modes. This does not mean they will always use the exact notes shown above. If you keep the same internal arrangement of intervals, you can start on any mode on any keynote. For example, here are the same four scales or modes again—this time all starting on the same keynote.

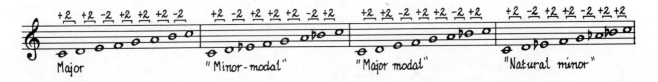

A good exercise is to practice playing and writing out these modes starting on different keynotes.

Other modes are used. Pentatonic modes are widely used in folk and folk-influenced music, and they are a predominant source of melody.

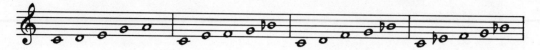

The ancient musical scales or modes can be found by playing any seven white notes in a row on the piano. Here are these modes with their old Greek names. (Indian, African, and Chinese modes are somewhat different.)

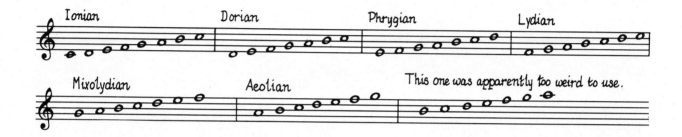

Once upon a time, you made music by staying within the mode in the melody and in the other parts as well. You will see that if you do this, you start to get some of the characteristic chord sounds of modal harmony.

Tonality, or key, is a later development out of the modes. Modal music preserves the sense of where you are by not going outside the diatonic notes (notes of the scale). Tonal music holds its sense of center through the movement of chords toward the keynote and keynote chord. More reliance on the chords means less reliance on the scale and a wider use of chromatic notes (notes not in the scale).

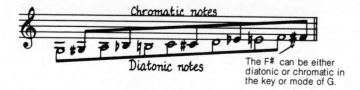

The F# can be either diatonic or chromatic in the key or mode of G.

Music of our time often mixes together modal and tonal elements. Chords from one mode are brought in to harmonize a melody in another mode.

Here are the four modes in G.

The following series of changes is clearly in G (and could be used with a pure G-mode melody), but not all the chords are strictly G mode.

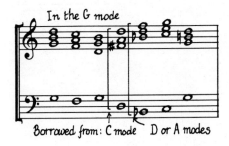

The keynote of a mode is known as the **tonic.** The fifth above is called the **dominant;** the fourth is known as the **subdominant.** Another way to designate these steps is by Roman numerals.

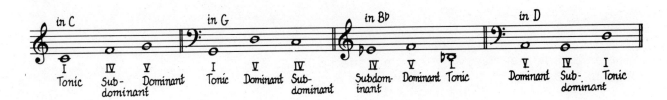

Triads

A **triad** is a chord made up of two stacked thirds. We have a triad on each note of the mode and we use Roman numerals to number them.

Major triads have a major third underneath and a minor third on top; minor triads have a minor third below and a major third on top. The diminished triad, which occurs once in each mode, is made up of two minor thirds.

Triads in C major:

In tonal music the melody proceeds by the scale or the mode; the harmony is made up of triads. Most, but not all, of the complex chords that come later on are made up by adding things to triads or by stacking triads on top of each other.

On the following page, we give the names of the most familiar types of chords as they are used in this book.

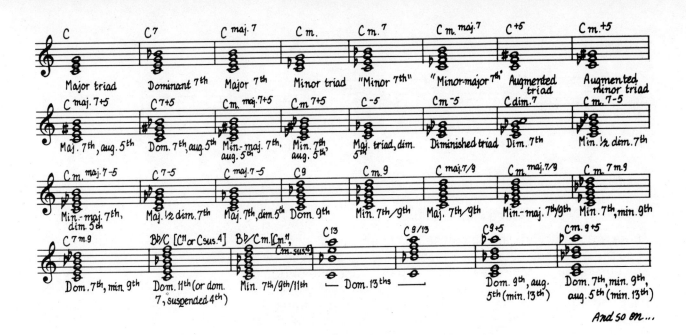

Rhythm And Phrase

Even a book devoted to harmony cannot ignore rhythm and melody. The connecting link is phrase.

A **phrase** is a musical sentence in melody, in harmony, in bass movement, or in a whole arrangement. Most of the time it is easy to hear the phrases in popular music because they are regular; that is, set up in 2-, 4-, and 8-bar units. The standard "pop song" formats are balanced forms made up of 16 bars (two pairs of 4-bar phrases or four pairs of 2-bar phrases). The so-called standard 32-bar tune is just a double 16-bar form. The other standard format, derived from the blues, is unbalanced, with a pair of similar phrases and an afterphrase. Each of these phrases is a standard four bars, adding up to twelve and multiples of twelve.

An older folk and pop song format consists of a pair of phrases known as the verse and a pair of phrases known as the chorus. Verse and chorus may have the same music ("Clementine" for example), or the chorus may be different ("Casey Jones"), or the format may be the kind usually described as AABA ("O Susannah"; "Home on the Range").

In the longer 32-bar tune, the B section is known as the **bridge** ("Jeannie with the Light Brown Hair" and "Beautiful Dreamer").

If the number of bars is doubled in a popular or ballad style the B section would be the bridge.

Typical 12-bar blues format:

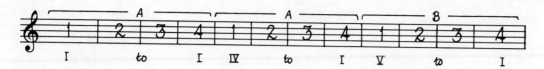

Twelve-bar forms on the blues model also continue to be common even in songs that have little or nothing to do with the blues: "Norwegian Wood" for example.

There are many variations on these basic schemes. "Michelle" uses an arrangement of 6-6-4 which adds up to the basic 16 in an unusual way. "Yesterday" uses a 7-bar phrase (the bridge is in the usual 8). Later songs and jazz compositions use overlapping and irregular phrases, meter changes, and freer forms. To be able to understand and put together phrases, simple to complex, you have to know more than how to count bars; that is, you have to know something about harmony.

In this book we are following conventions of classical notation used by writers and arrangers. There is no universal agreement or standard about how to write down folk and pop music which basically stems from an aural tradition—that is, learned by ear. If you really want to know how this music sounds rhythmically you must listen to it.

There are several common kinds of time in this music: 2 and 4, 8 (a combination of 3s and a 2), 3 and 6.

The way to tell 2 from 4 is by what happens in the bass. Earlier blues use an alternation of weak and strong with a bass note every other quarter; the feeling is strongly 2. When the walking bass appears, the feeling changes to 4.

The conventional time signature for 4 is C and for 2 is ₵, but the only sure indication is the music itself.

In both 2 and 4, the first and third quarters are strong beats. You can put an accent on the second and fourth beats, creating the effect known as **back-beats**; however, these are still called the "weak" beats.

I struck one chord of music like the sound of a Grand Amen.
"The Lost Chord"

BASIC CHORDS AND BASIC CHANGES

Triads

We start with a few basic chords and show how much music can be made with them. We will gradually add more chords and more changes in order to produce a richer and more varied music. The idea is to stay as close as possible to real music.

For a while we will use the key of G major.

The key of G major

I   II   III   IV   V   VI   VII   I

One way to show the relationship between the basic chords is in the form of a wheel.

Chord wheel no. 1

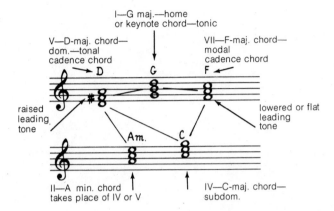

The Chord Wheel is intended to suggest the constellation of chords centering on the tonality of G. Progressions that move to and from the right side of the wheel are modal; those that move through the left side are tonal.

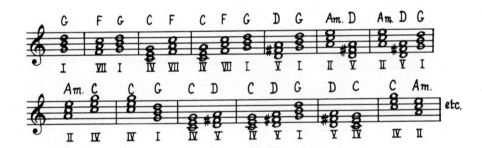

Here are these kinds of changes put together in progressions.

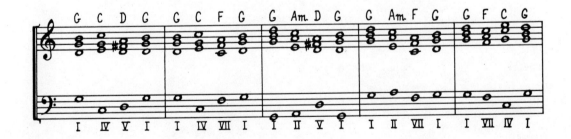

Notice that these chords do not appear in exactly the same form as they do in the Chord Wheel. Chords are "voiced" for playing convenience and for sound, depending on the instruments and voices used. When not otherwise stated, our examples are voiced for keyboard.

Voicings for a G-major triad.

Here are similar changes in 4-bar phrases (with endings or cadences) arranged like the chord skeleton for a song.

Song backgrounds are more than groups of chords that work together. Even though there is no melody, we can feel the structure of the phrases: groups of four or eight chords in a clear shape. Chords don't simply wander; they move in a direction and when they get somewhere they stop. You can feel where the motion stops: these are the cadences.

IV–I and VII–I are the most common modal cadences; V–I is the principle tonal cadence.

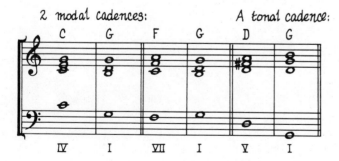

Another kind of cadence—the so-called half-cadence—stops the motion but leaves you hanging. Most of the time it is a cadence on V.

Another skeleton.

Modal cadences can appear in a tonal harmonization, but they are weaker and are not used in the big pay-off moments—the ends of the main phrases.

More progressions.

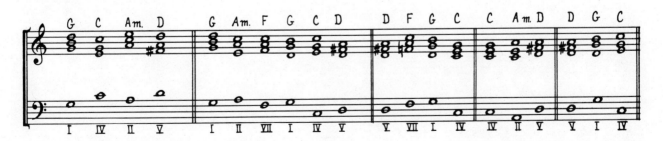

This modal cadence is very much used in British rock.

TTLT Beatles: "With A Little Help From My Friends"
           "Polythene Pam"
    Stones: "Honky Tonk Woman"
           "Jumpin' Jack Flash"
    The Who: "Won't Get Fooled Again"
    Traffic: "Empty Pages"

Two More Chords: VI and III

The Chord Wheel with VI and III added:

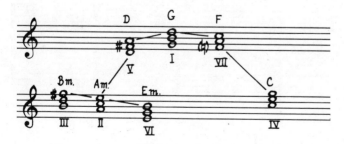

VI and III—E-minor and B-minor triads in G—complete the set
of seven diatonic triads.

The strong changes from III and VI:

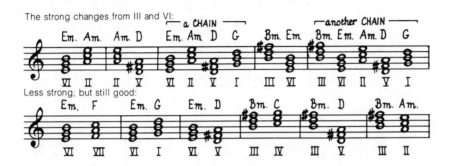

Less strong; but still good:

Changes using VI (I–IV–V–VII–II).

Changes using III.

All seven chords used here.

A great deal of music has been (and can be) made with these seven triads.

Hallelujah (A New England Hymn Tune)

Traditional

Another skeleton.

This is an "extra" 2 bars added to an 8-bar phrase.

Chords are rarely played in a simple block form. In this arrangement, the notes that are not part of the basic progression are played as part of the style (later we'll treat added notes as parts of chords).

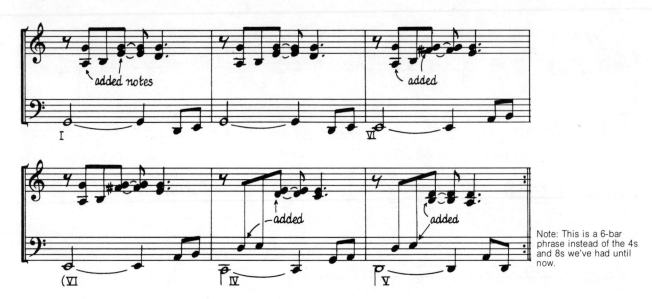

Note: This is a 6-bar phrase instead of the 4s and 8s we've had until now.

Sequences and changes.

A pattern of chords repeated on different levels is a **harmonic sequence** or **chain**. These basic harmonic "formulas" can make a phrase or even a whole tune hang together. They can be cut in and out of at various points and are, therefore, extremely useful.

Each measure has the same shape as the first in the sequence, but the chords natural to the scale are used.

If you made every bar an exact imitation, it would come out like this.

A **chain** is a sequence in which all the moves are equal.

Another sequence.

Standard chain going by fourths and fifths.

Walkarounds are short patterns that turn back on themselves
and are repeated without change.

Relation Between The Keys And Transposition

Any piece of music can be played or sung in any of the twelve key areas corresponding to the twelve notes of the full chromatic scale. Putting a piece of music into a new key is called **transposition**. Choice of key is determined by many factors, especially vocal range. Horn players prefer flat keys, guitarists prefer sharp keys, and pianists prefer C major.

The most familiar keys on the flat side are C, F, B♭, and E♭; on the sharp side: C, G, D, A, and E.

These are major modes.

Here is the Chord Wheel in the most commonly used keys.

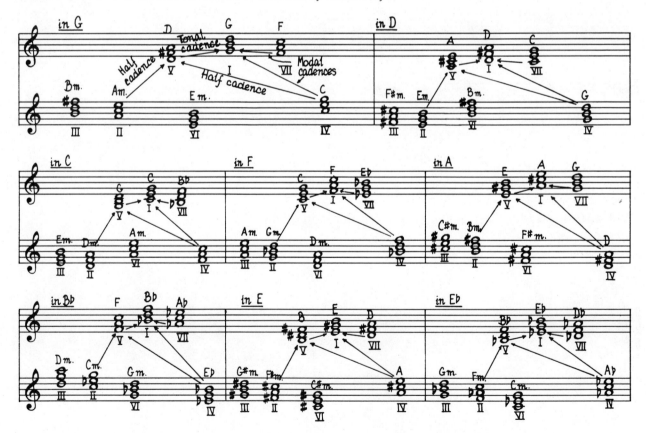

Anything that can be used in one key can be used in any other. The best way to learn transposition is to try out progressions in different keys, either by writing or by playing.

The most important link between major keys comes when the tonic of one key becomes the dominant of the next.

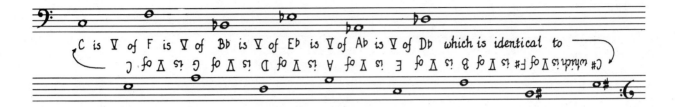

This is the famous **cycle** or **circle of fifths**.

Major and minor keys which share the same notes are **relative keys**. The relative minor is a minor third below the major.

Basses

We have been showing all our chords as if they were set for piano, with three notes in the right hand and one in the left. One advantage of this arrangement is that it shows clearly the two main elements of harmony: the chords and the bass.

Until now, all our basses have been the same as the name-note of the chords.

This doesn't always have to be the case. In fact, bass notes don't even always have to be in the chord.

G chord with F# in the bass.

The F#s and the D make a smooth fill between the chord notes.

Walking basses under the same harmonies.

Sometimes a moving bass pulls the harmony along with it.

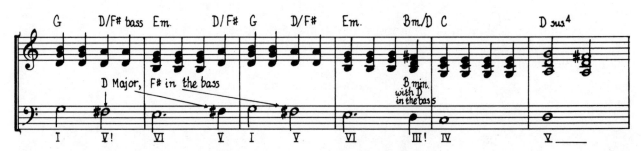

D Major, F# in the bass

B min. with D in the bass

Two chords in a bar! This time, the harmony changes to follow the bass, but the bass note is not the name-note of the chord.

TTLT Beatles: "All You Need Is Love"
Dylan: "Simple Twist of Fate"
Jackson Browne: "These Days"
Beatles: "In My Life"

All the chords we have been using have the name-note in the bass: these are called **root-position** chords. If one of the other notes appears in the bass, the chord is known as an **inversion**.

All these chords have the same notes but different basses.

Inversions are less strong than root-position chords and are used much less freely, but they are useful in getting from one place to another with a smooth bass.

A moving bass, especially one that pulls the harmony along with it, increases the feeling of harmonic movement. The opposite effect can be achieved by moving chords over a static, unchanging bass.

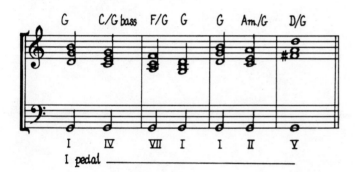

This sort of effect is easy to play on the foot pedals of a pipe organ; hence, the term **pedal**.

Chords don't fit together just as blocks; they must be fitted together, and the most important way of connecting them is by the bass. Making basses is part of harmony, and sometimes the bass line is so important that it drags the harmony with it. Good examples can be found in the blues settings of Chapter I.

From classical music.

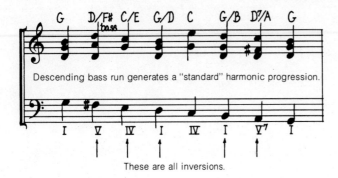

Descending bass run generates a "standard" harmonic progression.

These are all inversions.

TTLT Inversions
  Stones: "Brown Sugar"
  Four Tops: "Reach Out I'll Be There"
  Jackson Browne: "Late for the Sky"
  Joni Mitchell: "Free Man in Paris"
  Jackson Browne: "Fountain of Sorrow"
  Beatles: "Think for Yourself"

Pedal Tones
  James Taylor: "Lo and Behold"
  James Taylor: "Fire and Rain" (third verse only)
  The Who: "Song Is Over"
  The Who: "Live at Leeds"
  Beatles: "Got to Get You into My Life"
  Beatles: "Mother Nature's Son"

Bass Line Pulling Harmony
  Beatles: "Blackbird"
  Beatles: "For No One"
  Beatles: "A Day in the Life"
  Stevie Wonder: "Living for the City" (chorus)
  John Lennon: "God"

use Sat. night

Charles Ives *In the Alley*.
After a session at Pol's. Not
sung by Caruso, Jenny Lind,
John McCormack, Harry
Lander, George Chappell, or
the Village Nightingale.

The Dominant Seventh On V

One of the best ways to hear chords is from the bass up. Counting up from the bass, a triad is made up of a third and a fifth.

If you add a C to this chord, you get a **dominant seventh chord** on D; V^7 in the key of G.

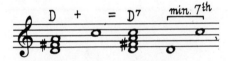

The dominant seventh is a highly charged chord with two dissonances.

Dissonances are unstable and dynamic; something must be done about them. Both dissonances in V^7 pull in the same direction: toward I. V may or may not move to I, but when you hear V^7 it creates a desire for I. Gratification of that desire is called **resolving** the chord.

As a result, the dominant seventh chord produces the strongest cadences which are usually the principal punctuation of the music.

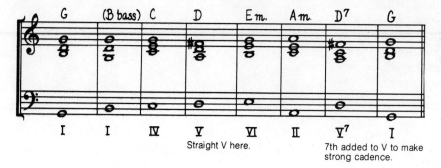

Straight V here.

7th added to V to make strong cadence.

The pressure of the dominant seventh chord toward the key-note chord has the effect of reinforcing the key. This push toward the key-note is the mainspring of tonal harmony.

All the other relationships in tonal harmony either strengthen or weaken this relationship. Two formulas that strengthen it—clinch the feeling of key—are:

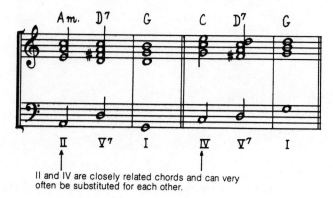

II and IV are closely related chords and can very often be substituted for each other.

Three More Triads

These are major versions of minor chords in the scale of G.

Progressions with major II.

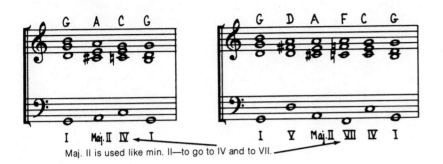

I Maj. II IV I   I V Maj. II VII IV I

Maj. II is used like min. II—to go to IV and to VII.

This combines both of these. *(optional)*

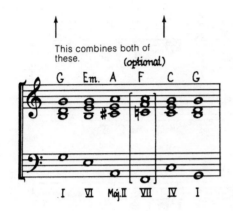

I VI Maj. II VII IV I

½-cadence on maj. II.

I V VI Maj. II

I VI II V VI Maj. II IV/V⁷ I

Here Maj. II goes to V⁷

I V VI Maj. II IV I

67

I–maj II–V⁷–I over a pedal on the keynote.

Major VI:

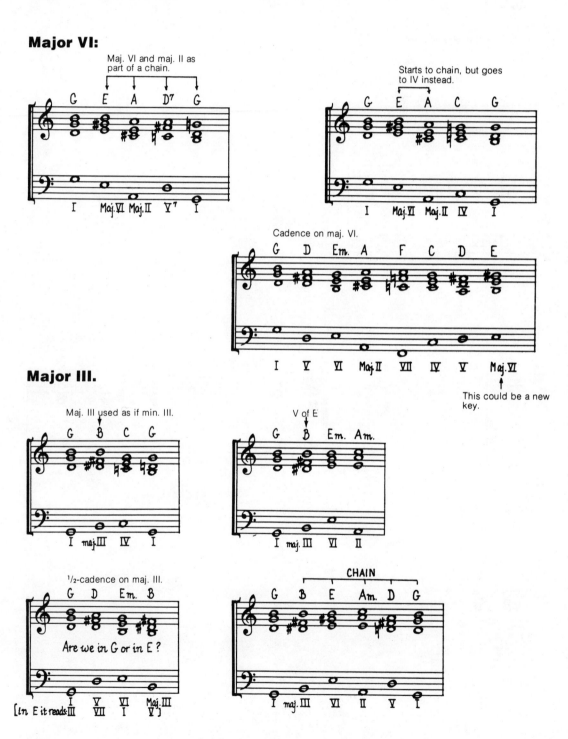

Here is a pop song bridge using all three triads.

V⁷ is used to mark the return of the tune.

These three chords can substitute for their minor counterparts that come from the scale, but when they do, they have additional potential.

Two Triads On The Flat Side

The triads on flat III and flat VI are not part of the scale we have been using, but they are used regularly to harmonize melodies in the mode, therefore, they're included in the Chord Wheel.

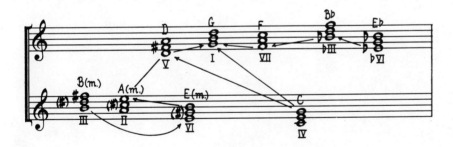

Common uses.

Try substituting majors for minors and flats for sharps in these progressions.

Some song progressions.

Lennon-McCartney: "Hello, Goodbye"

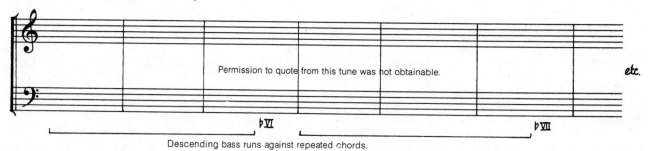

Permission to quote from this tune was not obtainable.

etc.

Descending bass runs against repeated chords.

TTLT John Phillips: "Monday, Monday"
Stevie Wonder: "Higher Ground"
"Superstition"
Steely Dan: "King of the World"

The Subdominant Seventh

IV⁷, the dominant seventh chord on IV, appears all the time in blues and blues-related music. It is used as a version of IV and does not resolve like V⁷.

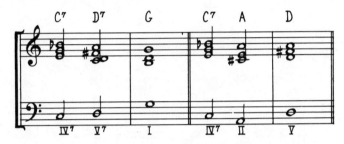

Two 12-bar blues using IV.

We were rough and ready guys but oh how we could harmonize.
"Heart of My Heart"

Secondary Dominants

You can put dominant sevenths on any note and most of them behave like V⁷, and thereby hangs a tail.

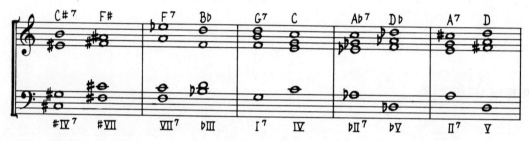

We have already seen that I⁷ goes to IV . . .

in exactly the same way that V⁷ goes to I.

In these changes, the bass goes down a fifth or up a fourth.

In the same way we can go from II^7 to V.

The dominant seventh is a chord with an inherent tendency to make a particular move—to a triad whose root is a fifth below. When the dominant seventh is on V, the particular move is to I. Dominant sevenths built on other degrees have the same tendency to move down by a fifth. When the dominant seventh is on I, the particular move is to IV; when on II, the particular move is to V.

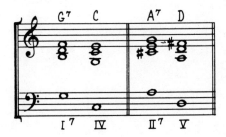

Dominant sevenths that move to other degrees of the scale besides I are called **secondary dominants.** Because of the built-in move they create strong cadences, and the effect is almost that of going to a new key. This effect of going away from the key and coming back is the essence of tonal harmony. How strongly the effect is felt depends on musical context.

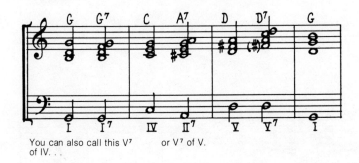

You can also call this V^7 of IV. . . or V^7 of V.

In classical harmony, secondary dominants are often described in terms of where they move. I^7 is called V^7 of IV; II^7 is V^7 of V.

This progression plays a musical game with your expectations. II⁷ makes us expect V, but what we get is not plain V, but V⁷. This sets up I, but what we actually get is I⁷, which has to go to IV.

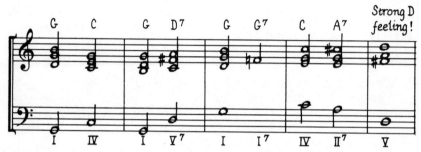

This time, a secondary dominant appears at the turn of the phrase. The secondary dominants in the earlier examples were details inside the phrase. Here, the momentum of the phrase is combined with the power of A⁷ to "tonicize" D—that is, to make you think for a moment that D might be the key.

What is the difference between "tonicizing" and "modulating"? When you modulate you really set up housekeeping in a new key; when you tonicize you get a mild sensation of change that is quickly dispelled.

The first eight bars of Scott Joplin's "The Entertainer" are based on a similar move to V, but Joplin gives us V⁷ right away and turns us back toward I.

74

Chord structure of "The Entertainer."

This, of course, is in Joplin's original key of C major. The scheme of the chords in G would look like this.

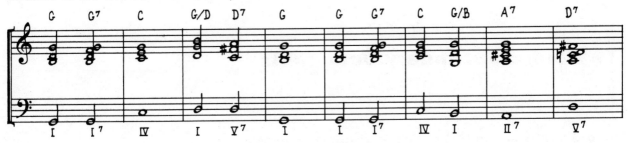

This progression uses two small cadences on G and then a big one on C. There is a rhythm in these phrases (..-..-....-) which brings a weight to the final beat even without the notes. This, plus the effect of the secondary dominants, underline the arrival on IV.

From rhythm and blues.

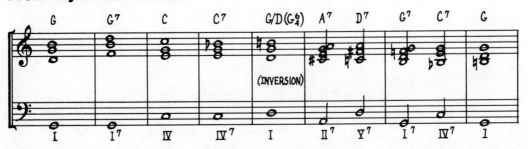

This example comes from rhythm and blues and uses IV^7–I along with the secondary dominants.

Here is a schematic picture of the relationship between these seventh chords.

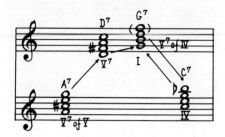

Two More Secondary Dominants

An old skeleton from the barber shop/alma mater closet.

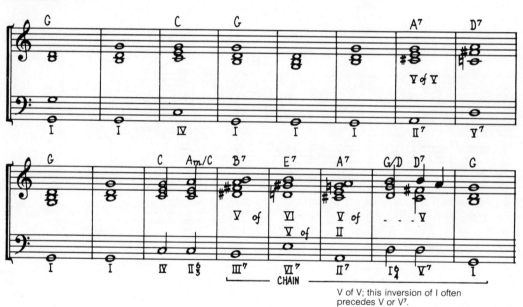

III⁷ is V of VI, just as VI⁷ is V of II. Very often, secondary dominants are leapfrogged together in chains like the above. Schematically, the new chords might appear like this.

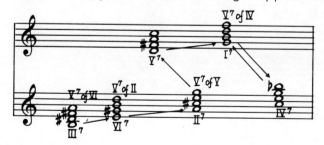

If you added another chord to the chain in front of III⁷, what would it be?

VI⁷ can go directly to II.

III⁷ can go directly to VI.

III⁷–VI is particularly strong because VI is the relative minor.

Lennon-McCartney: "Your Mother Should Know"

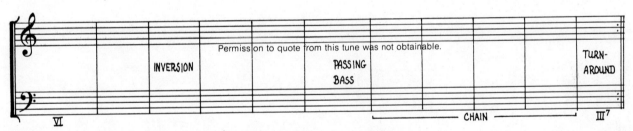

G major and E minor are closely related keys, and it is easy to slip from one to the other. The B⁷ in the last measure is not a part of a chain of secondary dominants, but a lead-in or turnaround back to E minor.

It don't mean a thing if it ain't got that swing.
L. Armstrong

Basses And Phrases

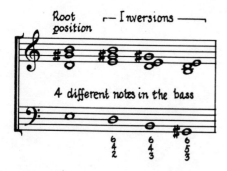

These are the classical notations.

Because there are four different possible bass notes, secondary dominants are very useful for matching moving bass notes.

Triads changing with bass movements.

Secondary dominants instead of triads.

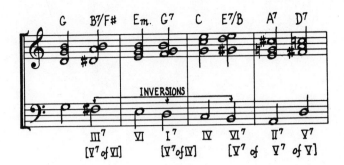

Secondary dominants can easily follow each other through the circle of fifths.

This cycle should be continued indefinitely, but it would wreck the key feeling.

Secondary dominants moving through inversions to natural triads.

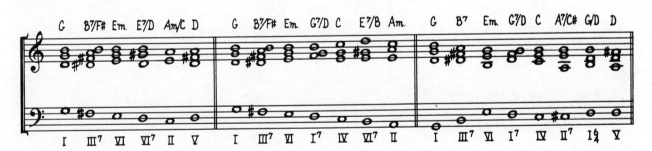

Similar formula used to tonicize D.

These bass formulas are not gadgets; they work within the phrase structure of the music. Tonal songs—from barber shop to blues—use common traditional phrase patterns with certain ways of going out and coming back to the main key.

	First phrase	I I	These two can
Either 4-bar or	**Second phrase**	I → V	be reversed
8-bar phrases	**Third phrase**	I →	going out (tonicize something)
	Last phrase	Chain coming back to I	

This is a typical form for a tonal song. The first phrase sticks close to home, the second goes out only as far as V (V can be quite strong), and the third goes out away from the main key (III⁷—V⁷ in the relative minor—is typical). The fourth phrase speeds up the harmonic movement and comes home—often with a chain of secondary dominants. Our barber shop/alma mater tune on page 76 is a perfect example.

Secondary dominants are essential to this scheme. The move to V is mostly made through II⁷, but it can be made even stronger if you do it this way.

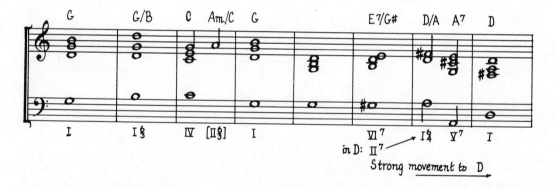

TTLT Bass Lines with Secondary Dominants
Billy Taylor, et al: "I Wish I Knew How It Would Feel to Be Free"
Stevie Wonder: "You Are the Sunshine of My Life"
Paul Simon: "50 Ways to Leave Your Lover"

More Dominant Seventh Changes

Dominant sevenths don't always go where they're "supposed to."

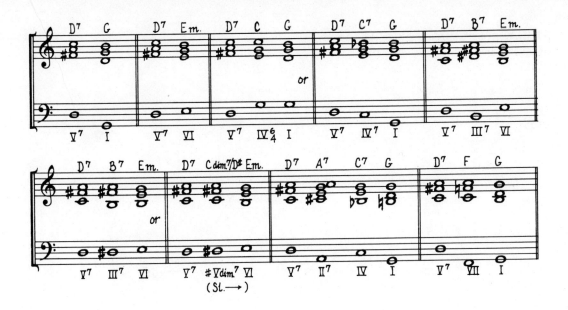

These are some of the places V⁷ can go. Any dominant seventh can do the same.

The Preacher
(old gospel in traditional form)

You would expect III⁷ to go to VI: it goes to IV instead. The diminished seventh is a chord that is used to fill the space between IV and I with D in the base.

More ways of using secondary dominants.

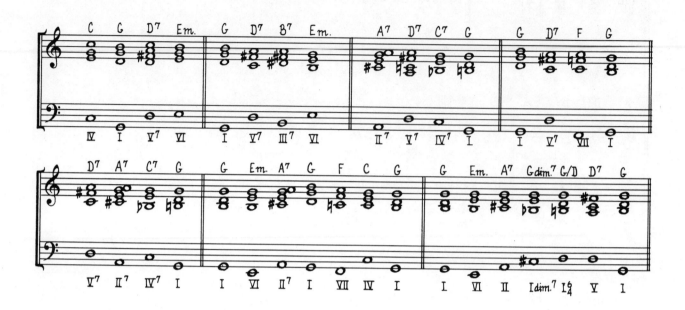

Lennon-McCartney: "Sgt. Pepper's Lonely Hearts Club Band"

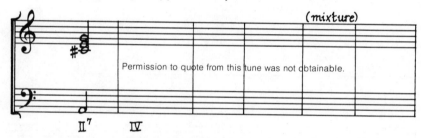

Permission to quote from this tune was not obtainable.

More changes using secondary dominants.

One more secondary dominant—VII⁷ to III.

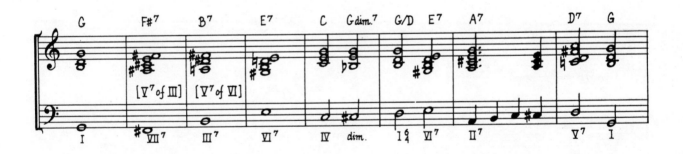

VII⁷ is not as common as the other secondary dominants, but it does turn up and doesn't always go to III.

I⁷ As A Tonic

I⁷ is regularly used as a secondary dominant going to IV, but the same chord has another meaning when it appears as a strong key-tonic chord.

The key-note or tonic seventh is stable and is descended from the so-called chord of nature, based on the strong overtones of any natural, steady pitch.

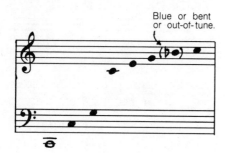

This chord coming from the overtone series is used as a drone or unchanging harmony in much third-world music and a great deal of Western neo-classical music. It is most familiar today as the **tambura** drone in Indian music, but it is also used in the traditional one-chord blues (see page 19). The note that is written as B♭ is acoustically between B♭ and A, and some people think that this is the origin of the blue note.

Voice-leading And Voice-leading Chords

We have seen how the bass can take on a life of its own; in fact, other parts can show a little life, too.

Here one of the upper parts parallels the bass:

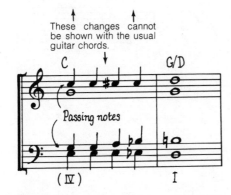

In this example, the parts are more independent, but they still follow the principle of filling in the space. The important thing is to make where you're coming from clear and where you're going equally clear. This works best in tonal harmony, and the stronger the feeling of tonality, the more filling you can do.

What is a chord? We are discovering that the concept of a chord is a little more flexible than we thought. At one end of the spectrum is the basic underpinning of the music which can be expressed—even played—in block chords, as, for example, by a rhythm guitarist.

From "The Preacher"

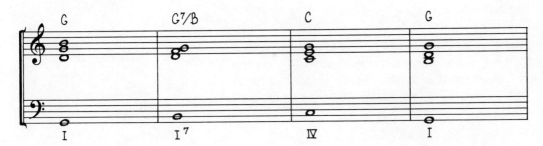

Here is a halfway stage on the way to being real music. There are more chords, but they are clearly elaborations of the above.

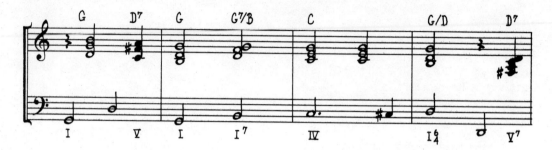

Next is what really might be played. The in-between harmonies are voice-leading chords; they are not basic changes and they don't tell you where you're heading, but they enliven the scene. All through this book, we will be treating chord changes on more than one level.

Some of these voice-leading chords are easily identifiable, and we could put numbers under them if we wished. Others are more like passing agglomerations, which may or may not "make sense" purely as chords.

Obviously, this is not really an F-minor chord at all. The chord on the third beat of this measure has more identity (it's on the beat and is a kind of A-minor seventh). Actually, there are no real changes here at all; V^7 goes to V^7 and the chords in between are fill-ins.

There is, however, some point at which in-between events can actually begin to sound like and be used as chords.

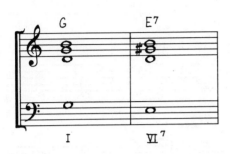

These in-between chords might be described like this:

The distance to be covered is I to VI⁷. Two parts move; the other parts hold through. The chord marked with an * is a special chord used to get to VI (or VI⁷). There is more than one way to analyze this chord, but it is probably best thought of as a voice-leading chord. There is a whole class of these chords which can be called slide chords; we'll meet more of them later.

Since this is a voice-leading or slide chord, it can take a number of forms.

These chords are like dom. 7ths, but they behave like slide chords.

Harmony based on secondary dominants is the common tonal language of hymnody, ragtime, parlor music, barber shop, gospel, country-and-western, early jazz, and blues. You can show the underlying harmonic identity by switching styles on top. The most extreme case we can think of is on the next page

O Little Town Of Bethlehem

Phillips Brooks and Lewis H. Redner

which can be persuaded to become this . . .

O Little Town Of Bethlehem Slow Drag

Michael Sahl and Eric Salzman

Same basic chord language in an old gospel.

"Yes, Indeed;" also "Who Threw the Whiskey in the Well"

Traditional
Arranged by Michael Sahl and Eric Salzman

On this same common language of secondary dominants, passing tones, and bass movement, the ingenuity of musicians has created a rich tapestry of decorative sonority, which is just this side of solidifying into a new and more complex harmonic language. The Twenties was a particularly rich period for a group-improvised harmonic style; everybody did what they thought was right, and most of the time it fit together dynamically because there was a common direction.

The results of all this individual initiative eventually get to be part of the common tradition.

Many of the songs recorded in this period were played in "head" arrangements—improvisations which gradually became set without being written down. Sometimes, they have the smoothness and the ingenuity of written-out parts. On the next page is our version of one of them.

Jazzbo Brown From Memphis Town

as sung by Bessie Smith

George Brooks
Arranged for piano by Michael Sahl and Eric Salzman

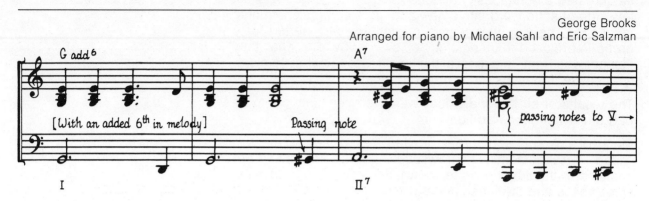

These two measures are really all on E, but the moving parts produce a shadowy B⁷ effect here.

Begins to move to D.

This dim. 7th is like a voice-leading chord, which puts a feeling of movement between II⁷ and I.

Voice-leading chords;

Top 3 voices hold.

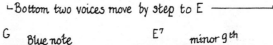

Bottom two voices move by step to E

This is Buster Bailey's clarinet break (based on harmonic pattern given above).

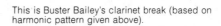

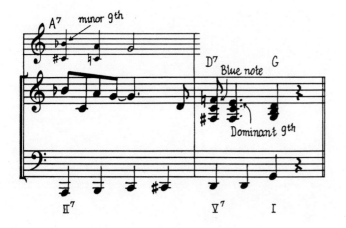

This is like the traditional song phrase form, except that the 2nd phrase starts with III⁷.

Come on; tune: if you can penetrate her with your fingering, so; we'll try with tongue too . . . after, a wonderful sweet air . . .
Cloten introducing the song "Hark, Hark! the Lark" in Shakespeare's *Cymbeline*

MAKING CHANGES 2: HOW MELODY MAKES HARMONY

Many typical kinds of American melody have their origins at a time or in a place "where there was no harmony." When you put harmony to these previously unaccompanied melodies, there is no set way to do it. The old rules of tonal harmony sometimes work and sometimes don't. New chords and new ways of using old chords turn up all the time and create an American harmonic sound. We're going to examine what happens to a melody when you put it through a lot of changes.

Here is a well-known folk melody of the Anglo-Irish variety.

"Come All Ye Fair"   Traditional

This tune is in a 5-note or Pentatonic mode in C.

This is probably the most ancient and widely used scale in the world. It came into American music from at least three different places: American Indian culture, West Africa, and the British Isles.

Tunes like this were created without harmony, but in the last two hundred years parts have been added to them.

"Come All Ye Fair"

Traditional
All arrangements by Michael Sahl and Eric Salzman

This old American part-singing style is a form of harmony, but it doesn't have real changes, and the bottom part does not behave like a bass. The melody is in the middle under a high harmony part (known as the descant). This style of vocal harmony is still standard in popular music from barber shop to rock-and-roll.

In order to make real changes and still keep to the feeling of the original, you use the main notes of the melody—the longest or shortest in each bar—and build triads around these notes. In this kind of harmonization, the important connections are between the chords and the melody, rather than between the individual notes in one chord and the next. Since there are a limited number of notes to make chords out of, it is assumed that the harmonies will mesh smoothly, and they do.

Although the melody settles on C only once, it seems to suggest a harmonic interpretation in C, with the end cadence on the dominant.

Arr. Sahl/Salzman

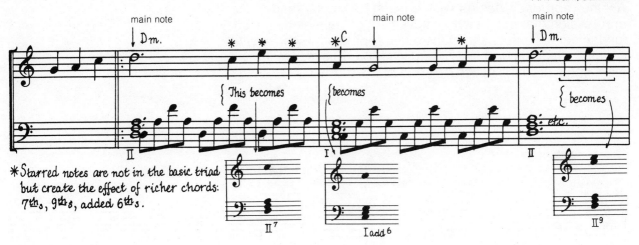

*Starred notes are not in the basic triad but create the effect of richer chords: 7ths, 9ths, added 6ths.

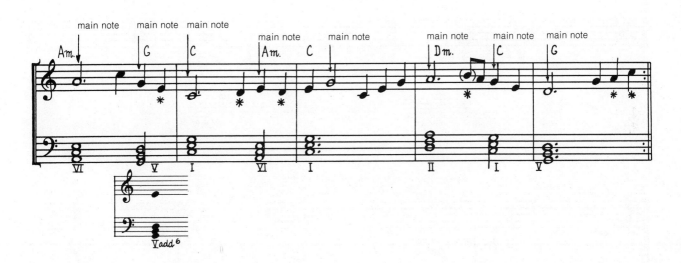

By following the main notes of the melody, this kind of harmonization emphasizes the phrase structure. The other notes do not require harmonies of their own; they may or may not be notes of the triad. They are, however, heard with the chord and add something to the harmonic effect. Eventually, these added-note sounds become chords in their own right; see small chords in above example.

Another approach begins with a standard, ready-made tonal progression that parallels the movement of the melody. This is fundamentally different from the other approach, because what counts is the relationship of chord to chord. This means that the main notes are not necessarily part of the triads at all.

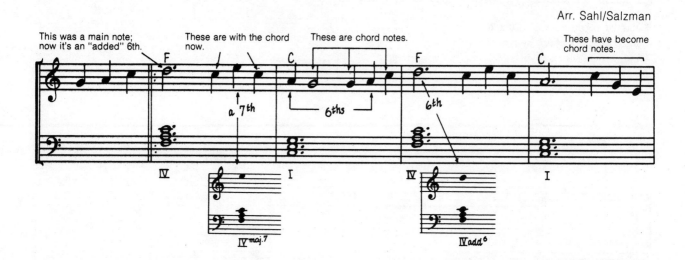

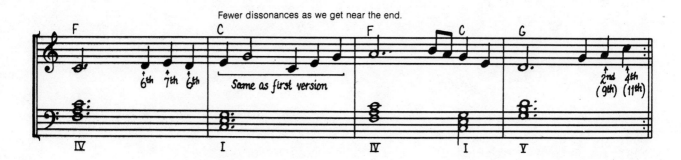

Here is a somewhat related scheme that not only uses more tonal chords, but is based on V⁷–I. The effect of the dominant seventh depends on the tritone F–B, notes that cannot appear in the melody because they are absent from the Pentatonic mode. Of the five notes in the mode, two go with the chord and three don't; any melodic movement at all will produce dissonances. All three dissonances—A, C, and E over G—eventually become normalized and absorbed into the dominant chord as V^9, V^{11}, and V^{13}.

Arr. Sahl/Salzman

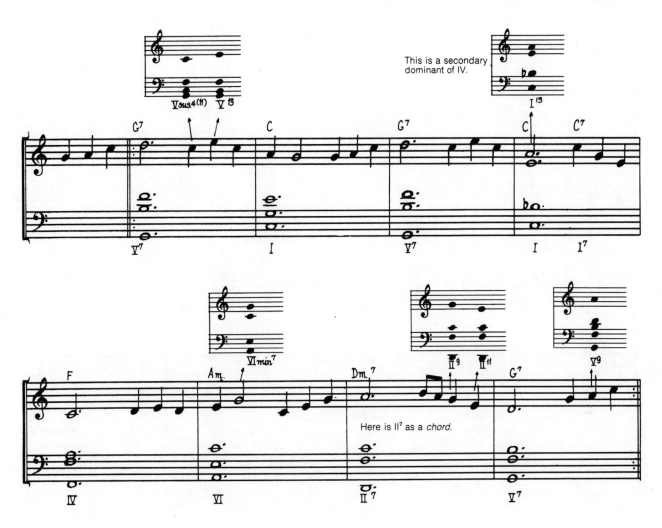

This is a secondary dominant of IV.

Here is II⁷ as a *chord*.

The use of dominants can be expanded through chains of **helper chords**. These chords behave like secondary dominants except that they are minor triads instead of dominant sevenths. Just as V^7 goes to I, II backs up V (or V^7), VI backs up II, and III backs up VI. Real secondary dominants on III (going to VI) and I (going to IV) are also used. Harmonic chains like this have a typical bass movement in fourths and fifths, and most of the bass movement in this example is of this kind. There are more chords and they both reflect and absorb more of the melodic movement, producing fewer dissonances.

Arr. Sahl/Salzman

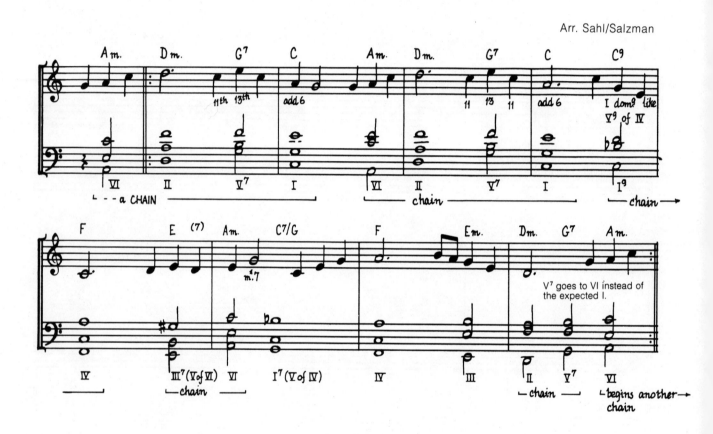

Combining subdominant and dominant areas.

This harmony, something like a blues-influenced popular song, has a real life of its own with secondary dominants and voice-leading slide chords. This secondary dominant feeling is so strong that it carries the same dissonances in the melody as V (i.e., the thirteenth over IV⁷, VI⁷, I⁷ and, fleetingly, II⁷). It also actually causes a change in the melody in one place.

Arr. Sahl/Salzman

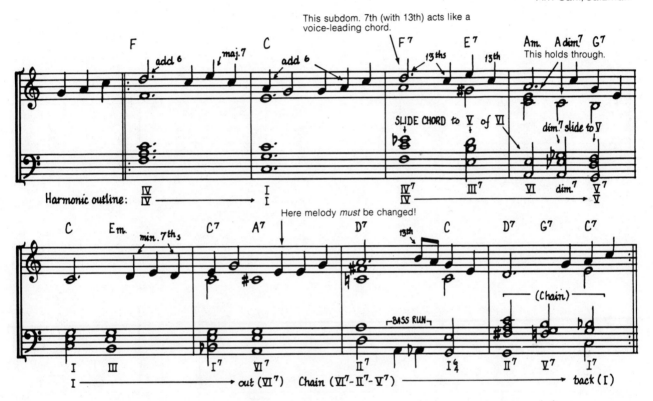

More chords and more notes in the chords.

Minor sevenths and dominant ninths now appear as full-fledged chords, and 7, 9, and 11 over V produce the special dominant effect often known as IV/V. Alterations and voice-leading chord effects are carried about as far as you can go without destroying the melody altogether. In fact, the harmonization is so loaded and attention-grabbing that the melody begins to sound like an afterthought.

Arr. Sahl/Salzman

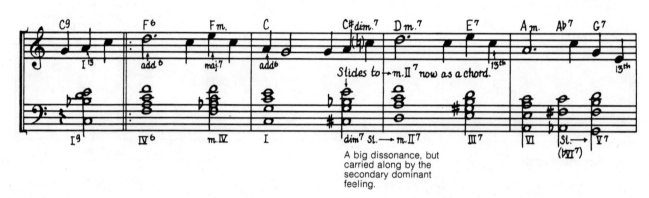

A big dissonance, but carried along by the secondary dominant feeling.

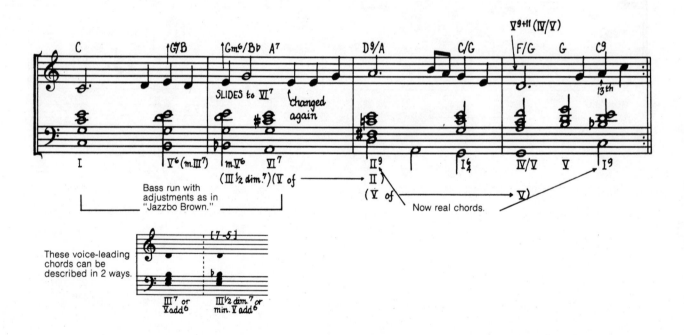

Bass run with adjustments as in "Jazzbo Brown."

Now real chords.

These voice-leading chords can be described in 2 ways.

102

This is another direction: one chord to a bar, but most of the chords have absorbed the added-note effects and have double meanings. With one exception, dominant sevenths are not used, and the cadence is made with a straight triad on V. The effect of these seventh and ninth chords without tritones is a softening of the strong directionality of the old formulas and a synthesis of tonal and modal feeling.

Arr. Sahl/Salzman

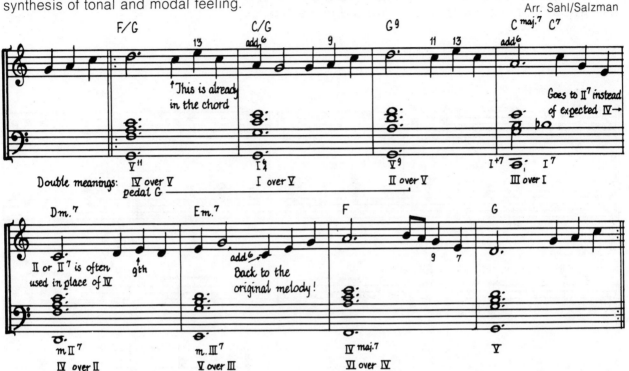

This direction is very characteristic of recent pop music. Here is a version that could be realized with a rock feeling.

Arr. Sahl/Salzman

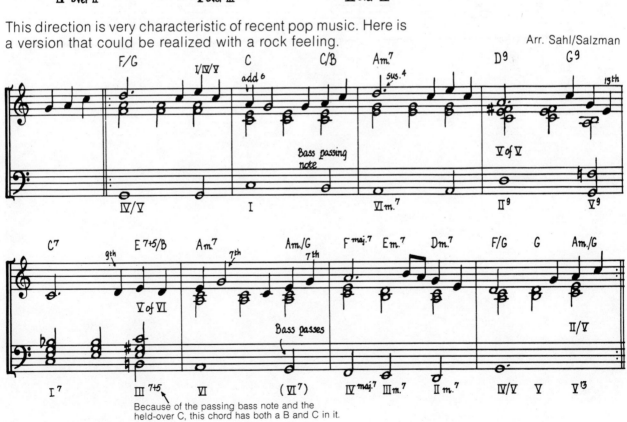

Because of the passing bass note and the held-over C, this chord has both a B and C in it.

Eventually sevenths are so completely assimilated that they are
used as freely as triads and even outnumber them. The strong
movement of the bass becomes an independent pattern that
doesn't even have to go to the tonic. We have blurred directionality and accommodated the modal nature of the melody. Here,
we have an upper harmony part as we did in the first version
on page 96.

Arr. Sahl/Salzman

When I use a chord, it means exactly what I want it to mean.
after H. Dumpty

MIDDLE CHORDS AND MIDDLE CHANGES

A tremendous fund of harmonic resources opens up through the simple process of adding notes to the triads and dominant sevenths. These chords, although descended from familiar chords, may work in different ways.

Sevenths In The Scale

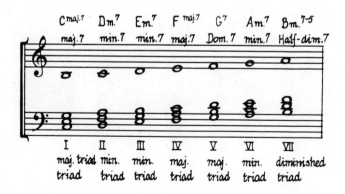

Here are the triads on all the degrees of C major. On top of every triad is a seventh; these sevenths are the ones that fall naturally in the scale. The seventh on G turned it into a dominant seventh—the only one that turns up in the natural scale.

Notice that you have to change notes—add sharps and flats—in order to turn the other seventh chords into dominant sevenths.

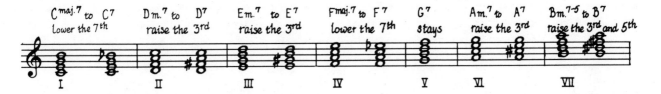

We have discussed dominant sevenths at length; it's now time to examine other kinds of sevenths. We just saw—in our settings of "Come All Ye Fair"—how these kinds of chords are created by the conflict between melody and harmony.

Let's take a sequence or chain of triads without sevenths.

This is a diminished triad (2 min. 3rds), which results from holding on to triad forms when moving through the scale.

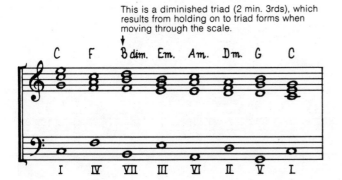

As we know, you can turn any or all of these chords into dominant sevenths and make music with them. But there's another way to go.

A chain in the scale.

The chain does not have to be used in its entirety; any portion of it is usable.

Kinds of 7th Chords in the Scale

Dom. 7th—maj. triad with min. 7th

Min. 7th chord—min. triad with min. 7th

Maj. 7th chord—maj. triad with maj. 7th

½-dim. 7th chord—dim. triad with min. 7th

Minor and major seventh chords are not as directional as dominant sevenths, but they often turn up in familiar patterns.

mII⁷.

mIII⁷ and mII⁷.

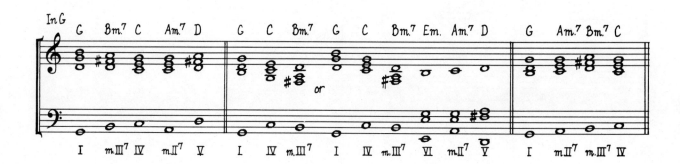

All the minor sevenths—all in G.

IV^{maj7} and I^{maj7}.

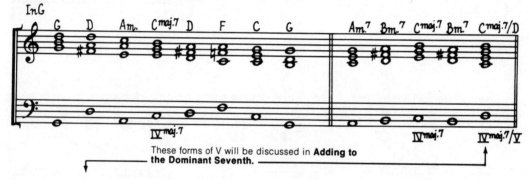

These forms of V will be discussed in **Adding to the Dominant Seventh.**

I⁷.

We're beginning to use other keys now. This example is in C.

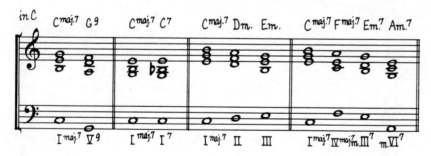

VII⁷⁻⁵.

The half-diminished seventh on VII generally goes to III.

110

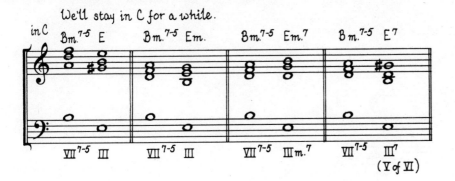

This chord also moves by step.

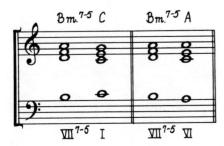

The minor triad and the minor seventh chord on II are sensitive chords that can be considered as substitutes either for IV or for a secondary dominant.

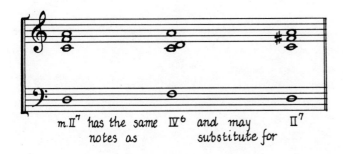

All of these forms are on the way to V.

Here is the standard progression.

Here, mII⁷ substitutes for IV.

Here, the first inversion is the same as IVadd⁶. Pop arrangers almost always call this chord IV⁶.

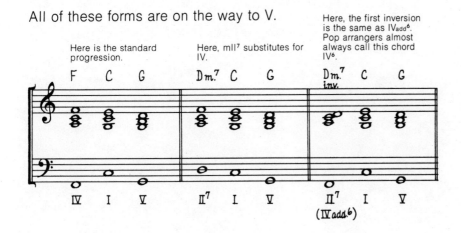

mII⁷ as a substitution for V of V.

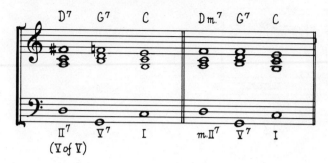

With this principle of substitution, you can make mixed chains of sevenths, some of which are dominant sevenths and some of which are natural sevenths from the scale.

Here you might be in some doubt about what the key is going to be.

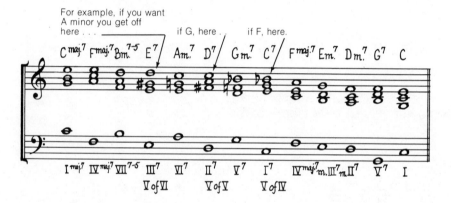

The chords that are natural sevenths here might be dominant sevenths instead, and vice versa, depending on where you want to go. These chains are widely used because they are not only pretty but also a tremendous convenience: they help get in and out of all sorts of places, and they can fill up dead space. Learn these chains in different keys, and experiment with switching the sevenths around.

TTLT Chains
Beatles: "You Never Give Me Your Money"
Doors: "Light My Fire" (intro)
Crosby, Stills and Nash: "You Don't Have to Cry"
Jimi Hendrix: "Hey, Joe"

VII–IV–I
Beatles: "With a Little Help from My Friends"
Beatles: "Polythene Pam"
Stones: "Honky Tonk Woman"
Stones: "Jumpin' Jack Flash"
The Who: "Won't Get Fooled Again"
Traffic: "Empty Pages"
Buffalo Springfield: "Bluebird"
Crosby, Stills and Nash: "You Don't Have to Cry"
Jimi Hendrix: "Hey, Joe"

Adding To The Dominant Seventh

As we have seen and heard, any note of the diatonic scale can be harmonized with a dominant seventh if it comes in the right musical place. This creates a whole series of new dominant chords. Such is the power of the dominant seventh that it continues to work the same way no matter what you put on top of it, as long as the crucial tritone is present.

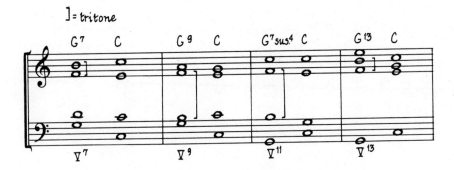

If the B is omitted from the G¹¹ chord, the C sounds as if it is going to move to B.

This chord is called V^{sus4} ("sus" is for *sus*pended 4).

Eventually, the C is accepted as a stand-in for the B, and the V^{sus4} moves directly to I.

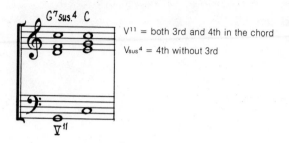

V^{11} = both 3rd and 4th in the chord

V_{sus4} = 4th without 3rd

There are other forms of the dominant without the crucial tritone.

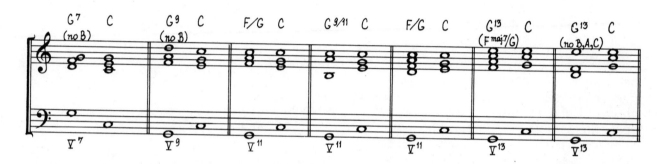

The higher you go in piling up sevenths, ninths, elevenths, and thirteenths, the more choice there is about what notes are left out of the chord!

The lack of the tritone removes the strong dominant seventh feeling but the seventh is still crucial. Any of these chords can serve as a dominant in the right place.

V^9.

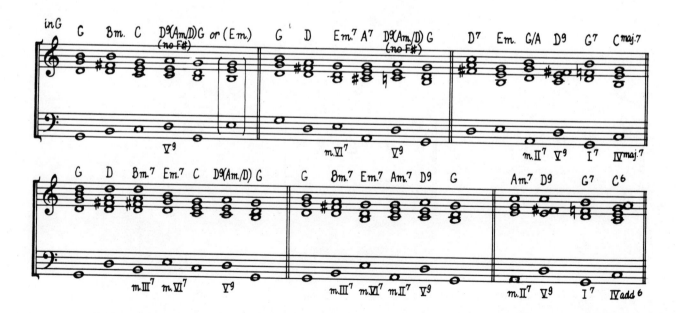

Forms of V¹¹

Both of these forms are sometimes called "incomplete" dominant elevenths because they lack the third. This means that the tritone—which is so important in the dominant seventh—is missing, and you actually cannot be sure whether they are based on major or minor triads. Nevertheless, they both have a considerable dominant feeling only partly due to the effect of the seventh.

This form of V¹¹ (in G)

combines the effect of the subdominant with the dominant.

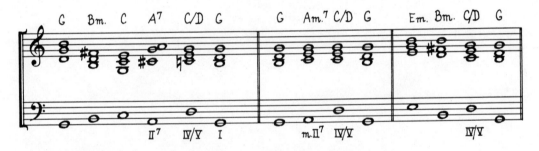

Because it contains the root of V, the seventh of V⁷ and the triad of IV, it creates a cadence by circumstantial evidence.

Eleventhts on other degrees.

These forms are used on other degrees like secondary dominants. Suspended 4 appears mostly on II and VI, as well as on I.

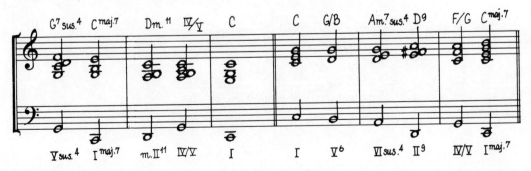

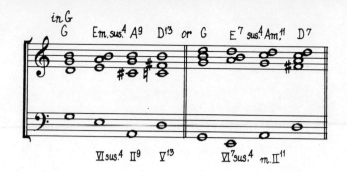

By contrast, IV/V gives birth to a whole gamut of chords with double meanings.

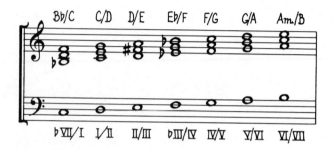

V¹³.

Very often this chord appears as a temporary sound, with the thirteenth (that is, the third of the scale), resolving down to a consonant fifth (the second of the scale). But with American melodies as shown above, the chord comes to be treated as if it had an independent existence, like a dominant seventh chord.

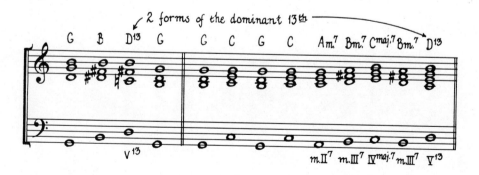

Anything that can be done to a dominant can be done to a secondary dominant, but some of these altered secondary dominants are more useful than others.

The same principle applies to secondary dominants, but the further they are from the tonic in the chain, the fewer of them are useful. The most familiar are the ones on II:

II⁹.

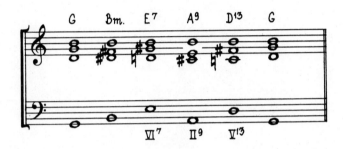

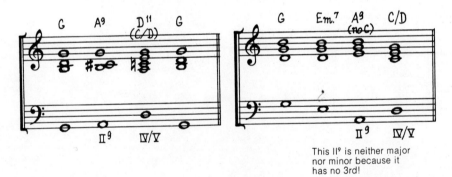

This II⁹ is neither major nor minor because it has no 3rd!

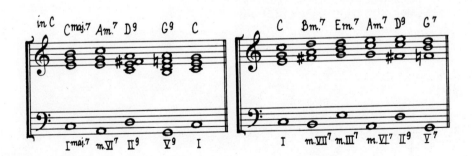

I⁹.

IV⁹.

VI⁹.

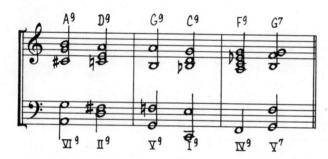

By analogy, other ninths, elevenths, and thirteenth chords can be made on top of any dominant sevenths (but not all of them are equally useful.)

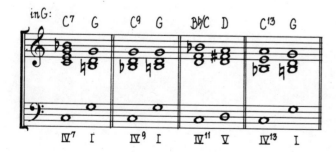

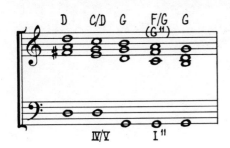

Jim Webb: "By the Time I Get to Phoenix"

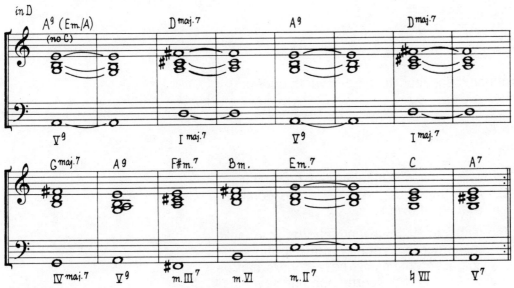

Chain of secondary dominant ninths.

Non-dominant Ninths

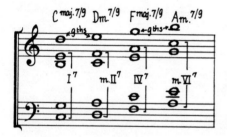

Ninths can be built on these four diatonic seventh chords:
- Major 7th on I
- Minor 7th on II
- Major 7th on IV
- Minor 7th on VI

The resulting chords are four commonly used non-dominant ninth chords. (All four of these degrees also have dominant ninth chords which we have shown.)

The effect of added ninths to these seventh chords is to make the harmony more diffuse and ambiguous, while at the same time contributing a coloristic shimmer. These chords can be used instead of or alternating with the corresponding sevenths.

mII⁹.

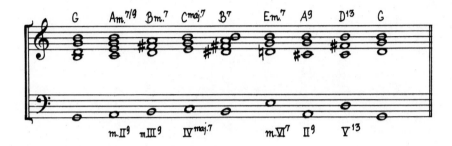

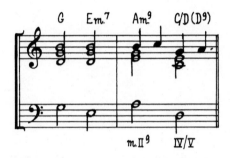

II⁹ is used as a substitute for IV$^{maj\,7}$.

As we said earlier, II and IV are very close together in feeling and in context, so much so that it is often hard to decide which Roman numeral or which letter to put down. What they share is a feeling of a "helper" area which prepares V. This can be used to prepare a secondary dominant and make it stronger. It also can grow out of the mixed chains, which, you will see, can be made of ninths as well as sevenths.

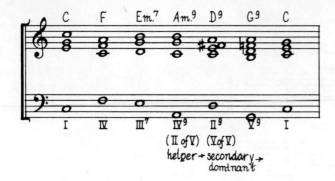

IV⁹ is used as a substitute for VI⁷.

This is the same trick as II⁹ for IV⁷. The mushy and rootless feeling of diatonic seventh and ninth chords makes it very easy to jump up or down a third in the bass. The feeling of the same general area is preserved.

VI⁹ used instead of Iᵐᵃʲ⁷.

We have already seen in the be-bop blues that III can take the place of I, or at least of Iᵐᵃʲ ⁷. All this shifting depends on keeping afloat by the continual use of seventh and ninth chords. One good, strong, old-fashioned cadence wipes out the whole permissive atmosphere, and you have to start over.

Seventh and ninth chords can be used in profusion without destroying the sense of a tonal center as long as the feeling of the chain or circle of fifths is preserved: bass movement by fourths and fifths and resolution of the sevenths. When this no longer happens and the ninths are freely mixed with other added-note chords, you step off into a kind of harmonic zero gravity situation.

Note that most of these chords can be described as a triad over an "odd" bass.

TTLT James Taylor: "Highway Song"

Diatonic Elevenths (Suspended 4) On II And VI

or more directly:

Same as above, but the E-min. chord includes the 9th (F#).

Added Sixths And Other Added Notes

Adding a major sixth to a triad produces a characteristic sound.

In spite of the dissonance, this chord is highly stable and can be used as a final chord. Do not be confused by the fact that the interval of a sixth and a thirteenth are the same; dominant thirteenths always have a seventh in them and are highly unstable; added sixth chords cannot have a seventh.

As we have shown, the origin of these chords is melodic.

A moving inner part over a static bass can also create similar harmonies.

Smooth movement of the parts with lots of notes held over from previous harmonies produces changes with a minimum of change.

Added sixth chords are not always used so smoothly.

In certain kinds of music, it is routine to "sweeten" the triad with the added sixth.

IV add6 is the most used of these chords, often appearing in conjunction with the basic triads.

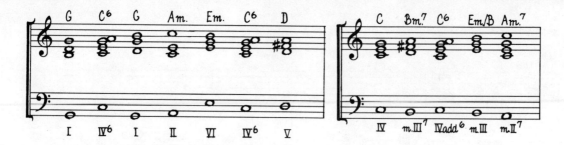

As we mentioned earlier, IV⁶ is really a stand-in for II⁷. In fact, these two chords have exactly the same notes, and whether this configuration is best described as an added sixth or an inversion of a seventh chord depends on usage and the whim of the arranger.

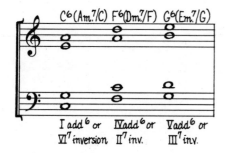

The added sixth on II is a very different kind of chord.

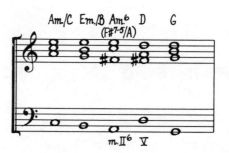

Putting a major sixth on top of a minor triad creates a chord with a tritone (C–F♯) that has very specialized uses: usually coming from or going to VI. This chord can be described in another way: as an inversion of the half-diminished seventh on VII, which we have already encountered in the circle of sevenths. The more we get into complex chords, the more we will find double and triple meanings.

TTLT Beatles: "Here, There and Everywhere"

126

We've already found similar problems in naming the ninths and elevenths.

Added seconds.

Is there a chord of the added second analogous to the chord of the added sixth?

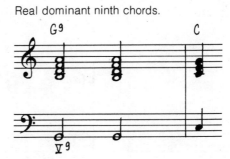

Real dominant ninth chords.

Without the sevenths, the quality of the chord changes:

Ninths without sevenths.

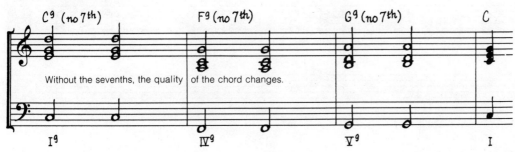

Without the sevenths, the quality of the chord changes.

If we play these in close position, we get a familiar sound:

Folk-style "added seconds."

The real origin of this chord is in playing style:

Instrumental decorations "Carter Family" style.

When dealing with the names of chords, it is always wise to remember that any system is a convenience, and it is not likely to be perfect for every case. Guitar chords, in particular, are adapted for the convenience of guitarists and may omit certain notes or realize the chord in a special form. The main thing is to know the chords as music and not worry about the names.

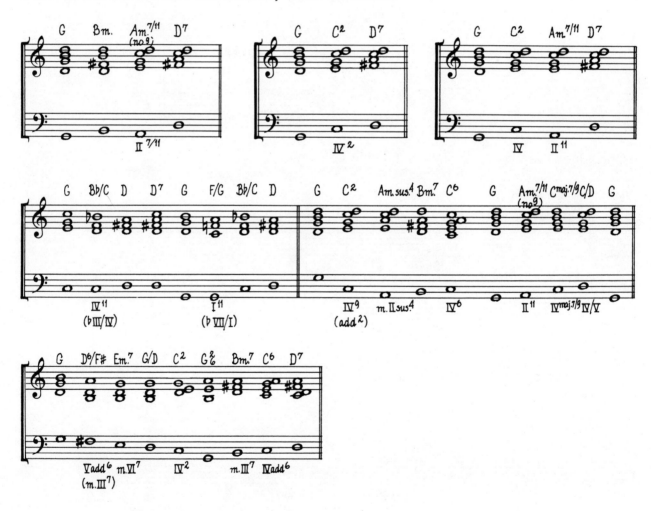

Another way to understand the origins of added-note chords is to regard them as melodic formulas rolled up to make chords.

These are the three principal Pentatonic scales telescoped into chords.

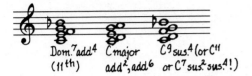

Dom.⁷add⁴   C major   C⁹sus.⁴(or C¹¹
(11ᵗʰ)   add², add⁶   or C⁷sus²sus⁴!)

These kinds of chords show up in banjo music and in modern classical music and are also part of modal harmony.

TTLT Traffic: "Smiling Phases"
Zappa: "Uncle Meat"
Zappa: "Oh, No"
Zappa: "Idiot Bastard Son"

Slide Chords And
Other Voice-leading Chords

In order to understand voice-leading chords, we have to look a little further at basses. Bass movement calls slide chords—and their relatives—into being. Bass movement sometimes fills up a musical space between chords, but just as often the bass is filling up the time.

Harmony:

Flats

Down

Up

Up and down

Down and up

The obvious next step is to get the harmony to move with the bass.

One way is to use inversions of secondary dominants.

Sometimes new kinds of chords can arise by making some of the upper parts follow the bass in step.

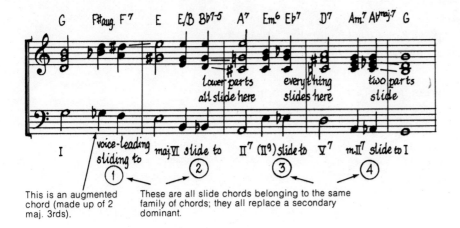

This is an augmented chord (made up of 2 maj. 3rds).

These are all slide chords belonging to the same family of chords; they all replace a secondary dominant.

These chords—all built on F—correspond to the chords numbered above.

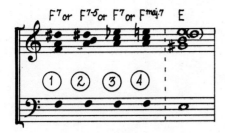

It is even possible to slide with a straight triad.

One part moves by step down with the bass. One of the other parts usually forms a seventh with the bass (sometimes written as a sharp sixth), producing a chord that seems to be some kind of dominant seventh standing in for a secondary dominant.

Slide chords of this kind have their own identity as chords and need not appear merely as passing events. In the above example, the last two are arrived at by jump and all three take their own full half-measure.

The slide chord in the first measure above is still another member of the family:

If we write it like this

we can see (and hear) that it is more like a part of a secondary dominant sequence on its way to A or A minor.

With a bass note on every beat, more and richer slide chords are possible.

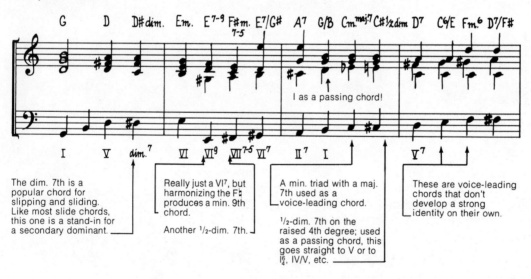

The dim. 7th is a popular chord for slipping and sliding. Like most slide chords, this one is a stand-in for a secondary dominant.

Really just a VI⁷, but harmonizing the F♯ produces a min. 9th chord.

Another ½-dim. 7th.

A min. triad with a maj. 7th used as a voice-leading chord.

½-dim. 7th on the raised 4th degree; used as a passing chord, this goes straight to V or to I⁶₄, IV/V, etc.

These are voice-leading chords that don't develop a strong identity on their own.

132

Fancier version of the preceding.

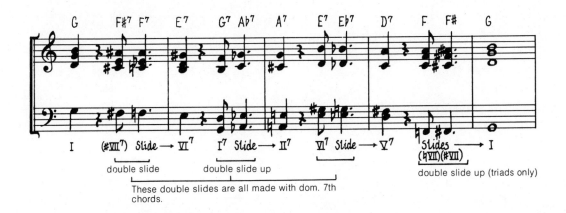

double slide

double slide up

These double slides are all made with dom. 7th chords.

double slide up (triads only)

Other ways of using slides.

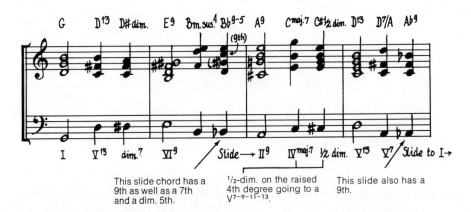

This slide chord has a 9th as well as a 7th and a dim. 5th.

½-dim. on the raised 4th degree going to a $V^{7-9-11-13}$.

This slide also has a 9th.

A **slide chord** is a harmonic sound piled on top of a bass that slides, that is, moves by a half-step.

All of these slides contain a tritone; the major half-diminished seventh has two. As always, the tritone tips the balance and makes the chord move. However, the tritone does not resolve the same way it does in true dominant sevenths. If it slides to another seventh chord, the tritones resolve as follows:

133

If the slide is to a triad, the tritone moves like this:

Slide chords are like secondary dominants; in fact, you can pull secondary dominants out of a chain and replace them with slide chords.

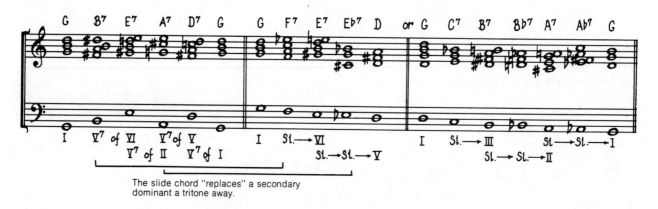

The slide chord "replaces" a secondary dominant a tritone away.

Sometimes, both the secondary dominant and the slide chord to the next secondary dominant can be used together.

All of the slide chords in the above examples are like secondary dominants. Lowering the fifth degree half a step—the so-called major half-diminished seventh—does not change the effectiveness of the slide.

Here is another related chord.

This is an inversion of another type of half-diminished chord—the so-called minor half-diminished seventh:

As we will see later, this is the regular form of II⁷–V⁷ in minor keys.

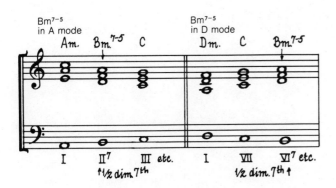

Both the slide chords and the chords they slide to can be inverted; that is, they can have any of their notes in the bass.

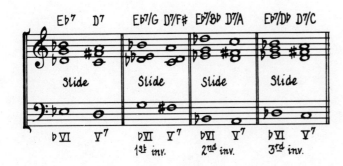

Slide chords (or the basses they're built on) don't always slide down. This step-wise progression can go either way.

The most familiar rising bass progression is this one, common from blues and blues-related music.

The slide chord here is the diminished seventh, a chord made out of three piled-up minor thirds.

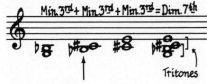

Min. 3rd + Min. 3rd + Min. 3rd = Dim. 7th

Tritones

This looks different, but sounds the same (aug. 2nd = min. 3rd).

Maj. 7th   Min. 7th   Dim. 7th
(also a min. 6th)

Note that the outside interval can be written as a major sixth (diminished seventh = major sixth).

The diminished seventh is an ambiguous chord, and you will find it written in many different ways.

The same notes!

Since all the intervals are the same size, it is almost impossible to tell one inversion from another.

All slide chords have some ambiguity in their nature, but this one is the most ambiguous of all. It has always been a popular chord for filling in musical spaces with a feeling of movement—even when there is little or no real motion.

TTLT Jackson Browne: "Fountain of Sorrow"
Loggins and Messina: "Rock and Roll Mood"
Grateful Dead: "Black Peter"
George Harrison: "My Sweet Lord"

Slide chords are largely interchangeable, depending on the melodic line, the style, the arrangement, the tempo, and so on. In slide chords, it's the slide that counts.

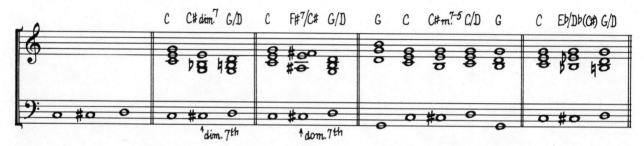

This sequence is often used to harmonize this kind of melody.

138

The result is a characteristically pungent harmonic effect produced by two tritones and a major seventh with a maximum of tension within a minimum of actual motion.

More descending slides.

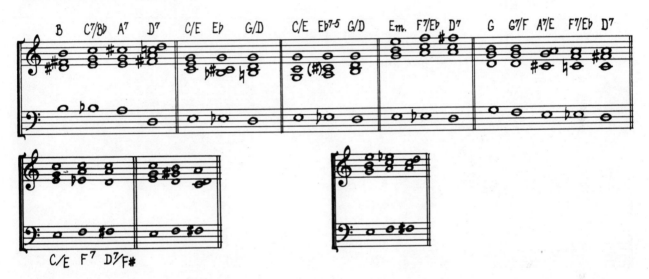

This is one of those chains that goes either way.

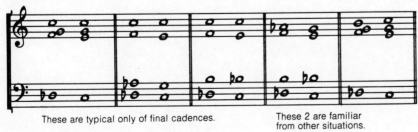

Slide chords can be used at the final cadence, but they have special forms.

These are typical only of final cadences.   These 2 are familiar from other situations.

This one is not used at the final cadence!

Slide chords in modern guitar blues are often on straight triads like these.

The E-flat chord in this example slides both ways.

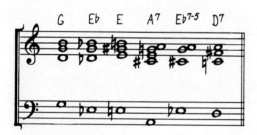

TTLT Beatles: "Honey Pie"

The ambiguity of slide chords allows them to be used in more than one way: any dominant seventh chord may turn out to be a slide chord or a secondary dominant.

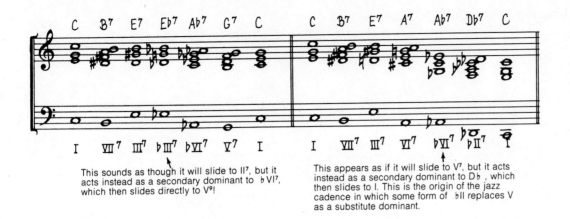

This sounds as though it will slide to II⁷, but it acts instead as a secondary dominant to ♭VI⁷, which then slides directly to V⁹!

This appears as if it will slide to V⁷, but it acts instead as a secondary dominant to D♭, which then slides to I. This is the origin of the jazz cadence in which some form of ♭II replaces V as a substitute dominant.

This acts like some kind of F#⁷ (VII⁷) going to III⁷ instead of the expected slide to V⁷.

III: Slide to II

↑This could be Bm. or even G.

. . . a song has a few rights same as other ordinary citizens . . .
Charles Ives

MAKING CHANGES 3: HARMONIZING A MINOR MELODY

"Pretty Polly" is a perfect example of American melody; the Scotch-Irish origins have been Africanized by a long stay in the South, and it is impossible to disconnect the blues from the ballad.

We give three different versions of the tune. The first two are closely related Pentatonic tunes; the last has explicit blues ornamentation. In fact, any sung version of this tune is bound to have small melodic variations in the blues vein which show its hybrid character.

Traditional

Traditional

Traditional

144

A tune like this in its natural habitat is not harmonized by any real changes. Here are three banjo versions that show the traditional treatment.

(Style of Rufus Crisp)

(Style of Ralph Stanley)

(Style of Dock Boggs)

Nevertheless, this tune can also serve as the model for dealing with minor melodies in a variety of rich, harmonic ways. Special features of the tune include:

> Three phrases rather than four (like the 12-bar blues).
> Goes to the relative major in the middle.
> Has no leading tone (so there's always an option at the cadence).

As we will see, harmonizing in the minor leads into many kinds of modal variations and chromatics; minor is a natural bridge to advanced chromatic harmony.

Bluegrass formula.

The harmonies are in standard 4-bar units, adjusted here and there to compensate for the melody.

"Pretty Polly"

Traditional All arrangements by
Michael Sahl and Eric Salzman

Another bass formula.

Either of these bass formulas could have been used for any phrase of the music.

Solving the melody measure by measure.

The most "logical" modal triads in the key (but the larger harmonic scheme of the three phrases makes itself felt at the cadences).

Arr. Sahl/Salzman

3-chord blues.

"Pretty Polly" has a blues-like phrase structure. The tune fits into a standard 3-chord blues by the use of mixtures, a ninth and a minor thirteenth at the final cadence. Of course, F♮ and C♮ neatly suggest the use of IV⁷ and I⁷, which is the "tonic" chord.

Arr. Sahl/Salzman

148

Dominant sevenths and ninths (but still modal).

The tonal ambiguity here is even greater. The relative major (F) plays a role, but the principal ambiguity is between minor I and major IV (D minor and G major). The D⁹ at the end of the second phrase sets up the cadence to G, which is a kind of turnaround to start the song again on ^{m}I⁷.

Arr. Sahl/Salzman

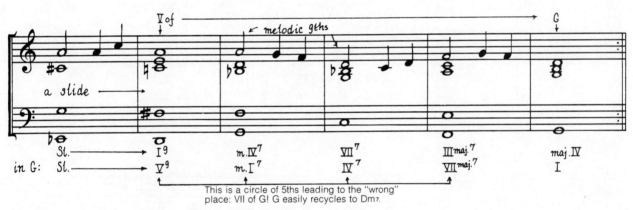

This is a circle of 5ths leading to the "wrong" place: VII of G! G easily recycles to Dm7.

This ending is related to the 3-chord blues with its cadences to I⁷ which is not only the tonic chord but also V of IV.

Secondary dominants and slides.

This is a tonal harmonization which puts all the dominant sevenths and slides to work. The first phrase (in D minor) and the second (in the relative major) hardly move harmonically at all except in the bass. The final phrase—a long chain of secondary dominants—is all movement, but always circling back toward I.

Arr. Sahl/Salzman

Chromatic bass formula in D minor (no real harmonic movement until SI→V⁷

Same formula in F

Secondary dominant chain.

Arr. Sahl/Salzman

The harmony is tending toward the relative major.

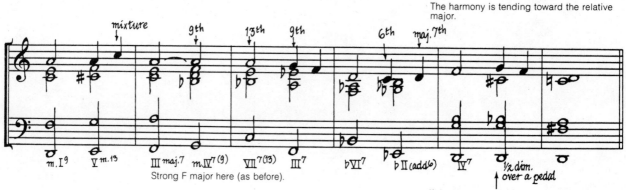

Strong F major here (as before).

If the bass went to A, this would be Vm⁹ (min. 13th).

150

Simple sevenths.

The sevenths and ninths help assimilate the melody to the harmony—you have a better chance of finding the chords you need for the phrase without running into conflict with the melody. On the other hand, the key sense is not so clear; if you change the first and last chords to $F^{add\,6}$ (same notes as $D^{m\,7}$, but F in the bass), this would sound like F major.

Arr. Sahl/Salzman

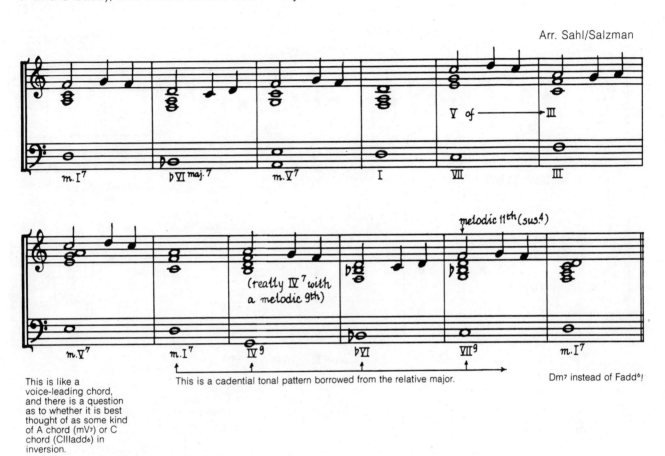

This is like a voice-leading chord, and there is a question as to whether it is best thought of as some kind of A chord (mV_7) or C chord (CIIIadd6) in inversion.

This is a cadential tonal pattern borrowed from the relative major.

Dm7 instead of Fadd6!

Moving to the relative major.

In general, minor tunes tend to slip toward the relative major, but this version does it more than most. D is re-established at the crucial moments, but the sense of home key keeps slipping away—mostly toward F.

Arr. Sahl/Salzman

Pattern in the bass.

The bass pattern is a movement in thirds. Instead of acting like a support to the harmony, it has a kind of arbitrary, geometrical character. Because of the number of options available in the minor in this style, it is possible to find changes that make the bass fit, even though it doesn't really contribute anything.

Arr. Sahl/Salzman

V⁷ with G in the bass and a min. 13th (F instead of E).

Try to work one out in fourths!

Bossa nova with ninth chords.

This version is in 8 (3+2+3), and the changes are pushed off
the strong beats, giving them a lift.

Arr. Sahl/Salzman

Close position chords.

Very often, a triad appears over an odd bass. The voicing insures maximum smoothness and the least number of surprises.

Arr. Sahl/Salzman

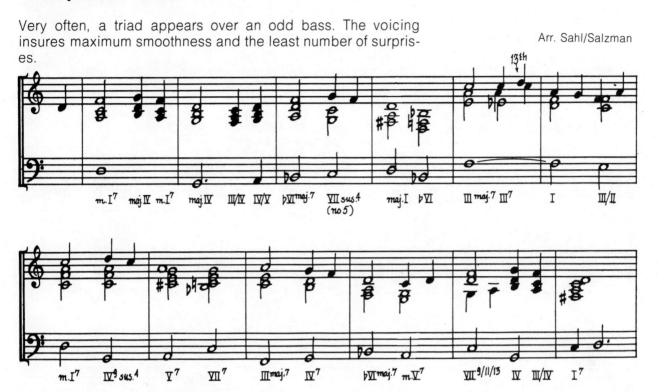

Chords from French impressionism.

These diminished and augmented varieties of chords were imported into American pop music in the Thirties.

Arr. Sahl/Salzman

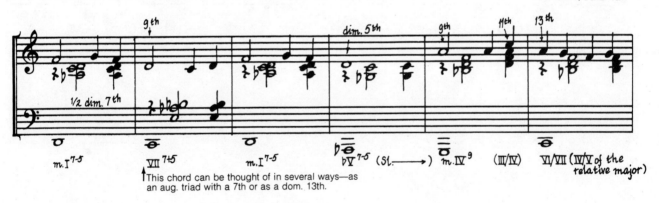

↑This chord can be thought of in several ways—as an aug. triad with a 7th or as a dom. 13th.

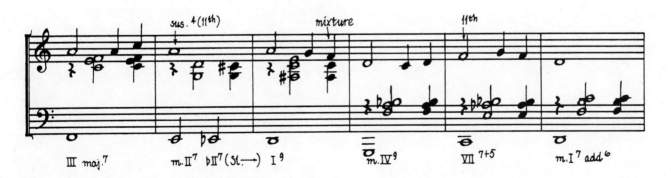

Ultra-chromatic changes.

On the verge of atonality. These are rich and complex chords that slip and slide. The bass line makes sense on its own. The chords are fitted in between the bass and melody with almost purely local voice-leading connections from one to the next.

Arr. Sahl/Salzman

Fourths.

Voice-leading chords built on fourths instead of the traditional thirds are still another way of diffusing the tonal feeling of the minor key. These are used in much contemporary music, including jazz.

The little black notes show the triadic modal harmony notes that have been "adjusted" to make the fourth chords.

Arr. Sahl/Salzman

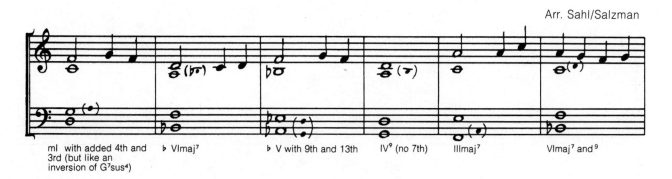

mI with added 4th and 3rd (but like an inversion of G⁷sus⁴)   ♭ VImaj⁷   ♭ V with 9th and 13th   IV⁹ (no 7th)   IIImaj⁷   VImaj⁷ and ⁹

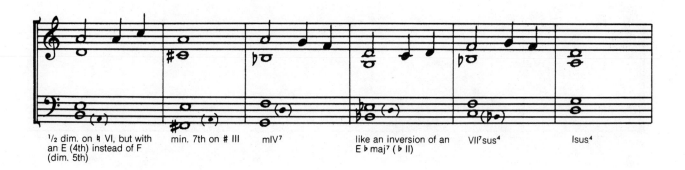

½ dim. on ♮ VI, but with an E (4th) instead of F (dim. 5th)   min. 7th on ♯ III   mIV⁷   like an inversion of an E ♭ maj⁷ (♭ II)   VII⁷sus⁴   Isus⁴

Modal jazz with a Latin beat.

Each bar contains an extra, decorative chord, some part of which moves. These inner harmonic shifts and the 3+2+3 rhythmic pattern work together. The decorative chord in each measure is marked by an X.

Arr. Sahl/Salzman

158

The last three examples are based on the blues variant version
of the tune.

Rock and roll (three chords).

Arr. Sahl/Salzman

Blues with secondary dominants and mixture chords.

Arr. Sahl/Salzman

A different way of "solving" the blues variants with emphasis on flat areas.

Arr. Sahl/Salzman

De gustibus non est disputandum.
Medieval proverb

ADVANCED CHORDS AND ADVANCED CHANGES

From here on we are treating mainly the musical language of the "sophisticated" pop song and jazz of the last half-century. We are dealing with complex chords and complex usages of simple chords.

It becomes more important than ever to read the music because the changes really depend on the way the parts move, and if the parts don't move well the changes will not work. Guitar chord names, which only tell you what notes to play and not how to voice them, cannot show you what actually takes place in the harmony. Therefore, no matter how difficult it seems, there is no real alternative to picking out the written notes.

It is our observation of human nature that if you give guitar chords you get guitar chords—that is, guitarists will take the easy way out and ignore the written voicing, which is the real essence of the music. Therefore, from this point onward, we will no longer give guitar chords.

Heard melodies are sweet, but those unheard are sweeter.
John Keats

Introduction To Minor

Minor is sometimes thought of as a variant of major keys, but in fact, minor has an independent family tree, and may have a more ancient lineage. The best way to understand this is to go back to the basic minor modal forms.

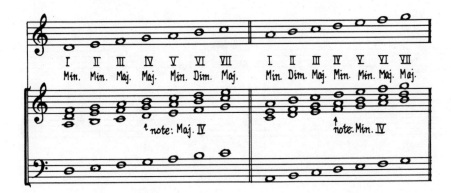

The D or Dorian Mode is possibly the most ancient and popular 7-note scale in music.

D minor (Dorian).

III IV V   IV VII III IV VII   II III IV   II V III IV V

Note: Major IV and minor V

Two Dorian harmonizations with modal triads.

Traditional
Arranged by Michael Sahl and Eric Salzman

I   VII I   III I

IV   V I   IV I   I IV VII V   I

Traditional
Arranged by Michael Sahl and Eric Salzman

V   IV   I VII   IV   V   VII   I   V

IV   I   VII   IV   V   VII   I

Of course, Dorian tunes do not always have to be in D. Here is a Dorian progression on A.

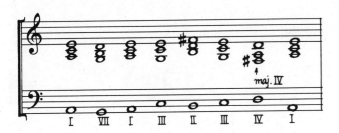

Notice that the modal side of G—the old Mixolydian or "natural G" mode—is very closely related to the D or Dorian mode.

In pure modal harmony, it is the phrasing of the melody that sets up the keynote; if the melody is vague, straight modal harmony will not clarify the situation.

Another way to show the relationships between major and minor.

Related minor to C: A minor (VI of C)
D minor (II of C)
E minor (III of C)

Related major to A minor: C major (III of A Aeolian)
F major (VI of A Aeolian)
G major (VII of A Aeolian)

Related major to D minor: F major (III of D Dorian)
G major (IV of D Dorian)
C major (VII of D Dorian)

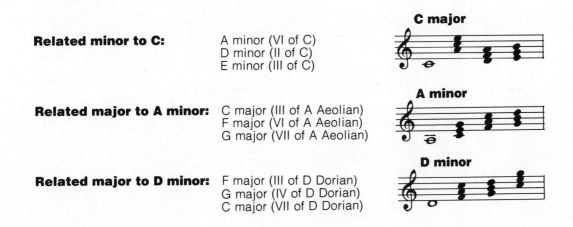

The A or Aeolian mode is the so-called natural minor in traditional harmony.

A minor (Aeolian).

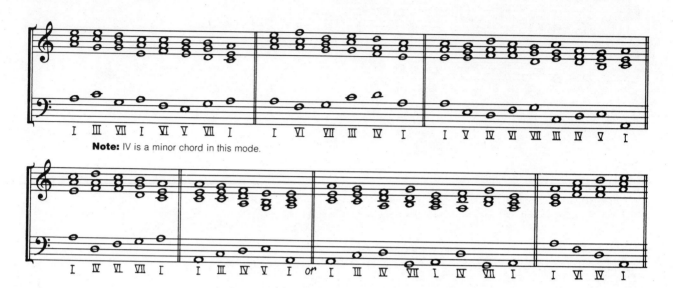

Note: IV is a minor chord in this mode.

Notice that in this kind of music the diminished triads on B don't fit and are not used. You can move quite freely between the other triads, and these movements have roughly equal harmonic weight. Chain movements in fourths and fifths occur, but they are not particularly strong. The biggest problem is to remember where I is, because there is no leading tone or dominant seventh to point the way. In fact, to our ears, these minor modes often tend to slip toward closely related major keys.

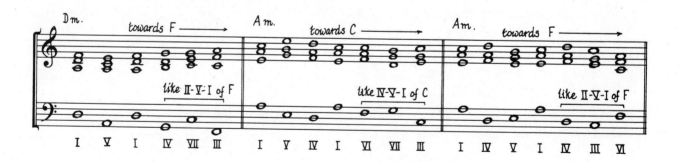

As we will see later, the ease with which the music can slip between the relative major and minor keys sometimes creates a doubt as to which key is the true tonic.

On the next page is a simple song background with only four chords, of which three—III, VI, and VII—are major triads.

(folk style)

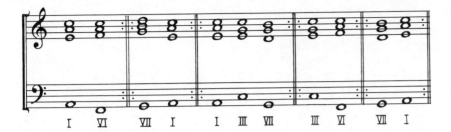

$$I \quad VI \quad VII \quad I \qquad I \quad III \quad VII \qquad III \quad VI \quad VII \quad I$$

Mixing the modes would produce two versions of the sixth degree.

Here is a Jewish folk song in the Aeolian mode. The cadential turns in this melody strongly suggest using a chord on V: in effect, a cadence on the dominant. The "natural" chord in the mode is a minor triad which has a disappointingly non-dominant feeling. One remedy is to omit the third of the chord and duck the issue. The other solution—which has long-lasting and significant effects for our story—is to borrow the sharp seventh degree (the leading tone) from the major.

Traditional

167

This is an old American modal part-song from Revolutionary times, which uses both forms of V in the Aeolian mode. The raised leading tone is used at the cadences, producing not only a strong dominant but, at one point, an augmented triad (two major thirds). Otherwise minor V is used or the third is omitted. The natural chord on II—the diminished triad made up of two minor thirds—is also used and it goes both to I and III; sometimes this appears in the form of a minor third, B–D, with no F. This is music for part-singing, and the life of the parts helps create the harmonies.

William Billings: David's Lamentation

Dominants And Dominant Sevenths In The Minor

Modal minors often use a major triad or dominant seventh on V.

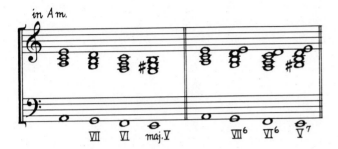

The dominant seventh effect in modal minor harmony of this kind is often saved for a crucial point: a turnaround (return to the main melody) or other important move is strongly defined by the directional push of the dominant seventh.

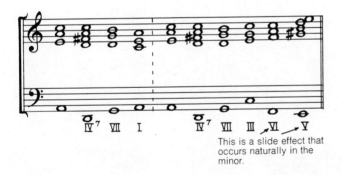

This is a slide effect that occurs naturally in the minor.

With real dominants and dominant sevenths in the picture, secondary dominants can also be brought into play.

Most of this sequence is really in the relative major (III).

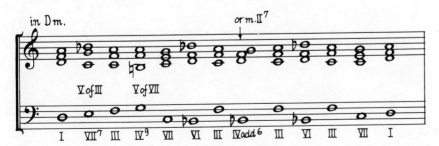

This tends toward the relative major all the time, but never quite gets there.

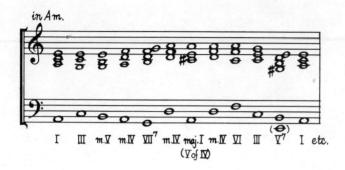

The pattern of secondary dominants here works like this
to→I
to→IV
to→III
V⁷ turnaround

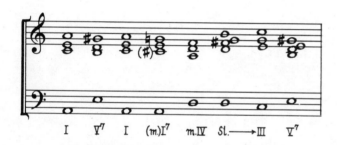

The diminished triad or I or VI⁷ functions like the subdom. 7th

---

TTLT Pete Seeger: "Waist Deep in the Big Muddy"

170

With the use of secondary dominants, the whole technique of
tonal harmony comes into play in the minor.

Bobby Hebb: "Sunny"

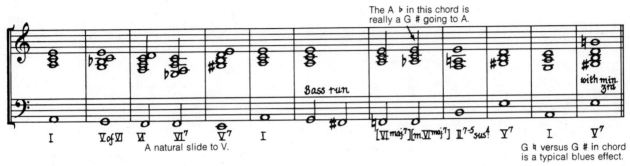

Notice that VI⁷ slides naturally (in Aeolian minor) to V or V⁷.

Classic tonal minor progressions can be found in the early
ragtimes where they are used with great skill.

"Pegasus"

(James Scott)

Here is the first strain of "Ragtime Nightingale" by Joseph Lamb.

The half-diminished seventh on II—the "natural" form of II in the key—turns out to be the pivot chord between the minor and the relative major.

Tonal And Modal In Minor

If you take the tonal relationships we have studied in major and lay them on the modal relationships of minor keys, you get a series of relationships that make the Minor Chord Wheel much more complicated than the Major Chord Wheel.

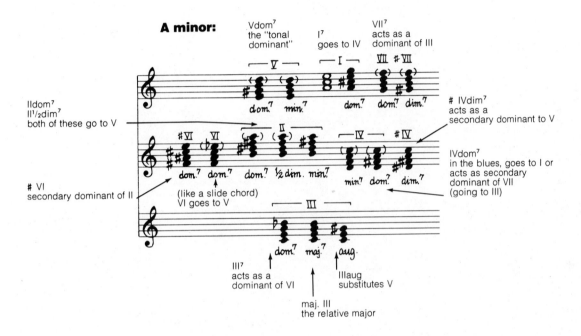

Learn these chords in the other common minor keys!

Main Tonal Movements In The Minor

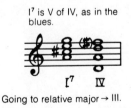

I^7 is V of IV, as in the blues.

Going to relative major → III.

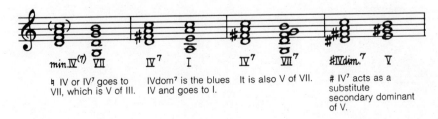

♮ IV or IV^7 goes to VII, which is V of III.

$IVdom^7$ is the blues IV and goes to I.

It is also V of VII.

IV^7 acts as a substitute secondary dominant of V.

Strung together:

I I⁷ IV IV⁷ I⁷ IV VII⁷ III IV #IVdim.⁷ V

Uses of VI, II, and V in the minor.

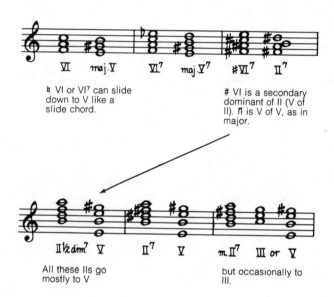

VI maj.V   VI⁷ maj.V⁷   #VI⁷ II⁷

♮ VI or VI⁷ can slide
down to V like a
slide chord.

VI is a secondary
dominant of II (V of
II). II is V of V, as in
major.

II½dim⁷ V   II⁷ V   m.II⁷ III or V

All these IIs go
mostly to V

but occasionally to
III.

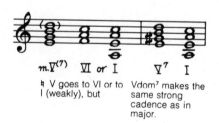

m.V⁽⁷⁾ VI or I   V⁷ I

♮ V goes to VI or to
I (weakly), but

Vdom⁷ makes the
same strong
cadence as in
major.

Strung together:

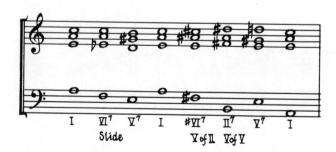

I VI⁷ V⁷ I #VI⁷ II⁷ V⁷ I
   Slide   V of II V of V

174

Uses of VII and III in the minor.

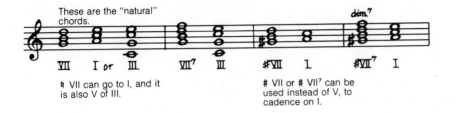

♮ VII can go to I, and it is also V of III.

VII or # VII⁷ can be used instead of V, to cadence on I.

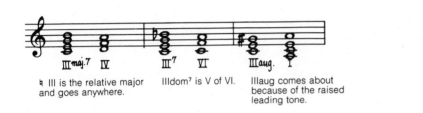

♮ III is the relative major and goes anywhere.

IIIdom⁷ is V of VI.

IIIaug comes about because of the raised leading tone.

Strung together:

Preparing V In Minor

The great problem in minor is to define the key with clarity. In traditional tonal minor, the trick is to get to the dominant—major V or V⁷, neither of which exists in the natural minor scale with its lowered seventh degree—and to get there without destroying the minor feeling. The basic bass movements are similar to major.

but there are more chord possibilities.

All these are approach chords to the dominant.

On IV:

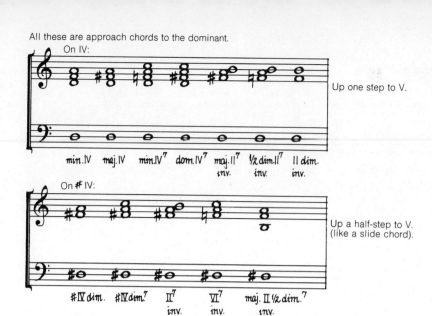

Up one step to V.

min. IV   maj. IV   min. IV⁷   dom. IV⁷   maj. II⁷ inv.   ½ dim. II⁷ inv.   II dim. inv.

On #IV:

Up a half-step to V.
(like a slide chord).

#IV dim.   #IV dim.⁷   II⁷ inv.   VI⁷ inv.   maj. II ½ dim.⁷ inv.

On VI:

Down a half-step to V
(like a slide chord).

VI   VI⁷   II ½ dim.⁷ inv.   VI add⁶   maj. II ½ dim.⁷ inv.

On II:

Up a fourth to V.

II dim.   II ½ dim.⁷   m. II⁷   II dom.⁷   maj. II ½ dim.⁷

A few typical ways of getting to V.

I   II ½ dim.   V⁷   I

#VI⁷   II   V⁷

III⁷   II ½ dim.   V

I   III   IV   V

IV   III⁷   V⁷

I   m. V   VI ½ dim. V

II ½ dim. dim.⁷   V

176

Preparing Other Degrees

Once you accept these chords as preparing the dominant, it is a very small step to hearing their equivalent numbers going to the two other important dominants in the minor: major II or II⁷ (V of V),

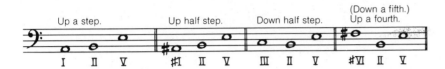

and VII or VII⁷ (V of III, the relative major).

The distance from III back to I is not far, because III leads easily into V or into three of the four basses that prepare V.

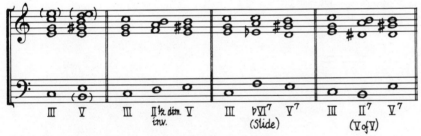

You can use the other chords on these basses, too.

III goes to II the same way that VI goes to V; in the process, you can alter III into the various approach chords.

Preparing II⁷ (on the way to V).

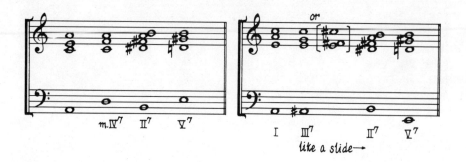

Preparing III (relative major).

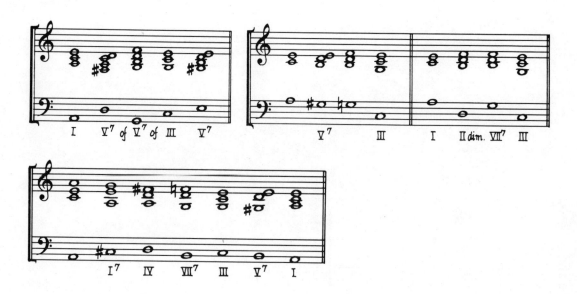

Preparing II⁷ and III.

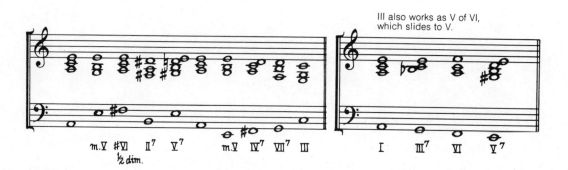

Minor progressions with secondary dominants.

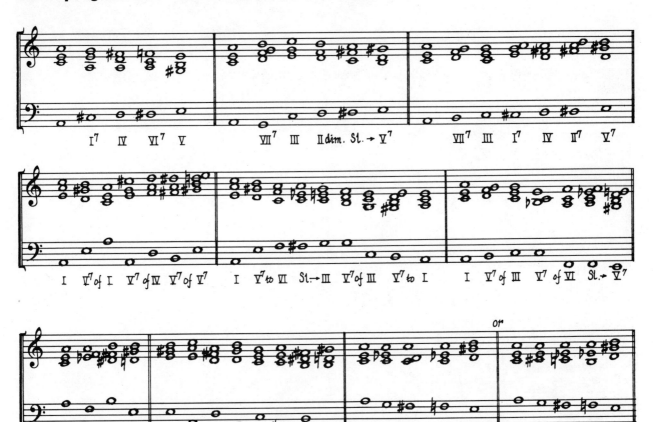

Diminished And Augmented Triads

There are two kinds of triads about which we have said very little. The pure diminished triad, made up of two major thirds, occurs naturally on the seventh (or "leading tone") degree in major and minor and on a couple of other places in minor.

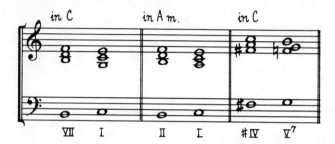

Pure diminished triads are rare; they tend to be absorbed into various kinds of sevenths.

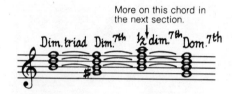

Augmented triads are made up of two major thirds. An augmented triad occurs on the third degree in minor, and it turns up in major keys as a voice-leading chord.

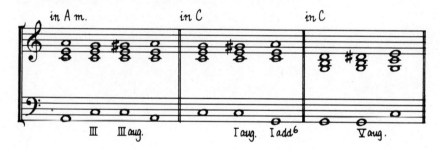

Augmented chords also show up, although somewhat less commonly, in seventh chords.

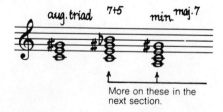

TTLT Beatles: "I Want You (She's So Heavy)"
Beatles: "Something"
Beatles: "Strawberry Fields Forever"

More Kinds Of Sevenths

We are already familiar with the so-called half-diminished sevenths—for example,

on the second degree in minor.

Unlike the dominant seventh, this chord has two minor thirds with a major third on top: the outer interval is, of course, a minor seventh, and there is a tritone in the middle.

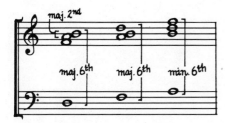

These chords have the same notes but very different qualities, and they are often used in different ways.

Notice that when this chord appears in different positions (in different voicings and in inversions with other bass notes as above), the minor seventh turns into a major second, the minor third becomes a major sixth, and the major third inverts to a minor sixth.

These chords sometimes function as genuine II chords, but sometimes they slide.

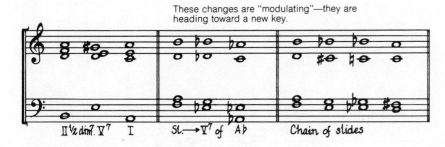

These changes are "modulating"—they are heading toward a new key.

The term half-diminished refers to the fact that these chords contain a diminished triad: B–D–F. The full-diminished chord—with Ab—is, of course, the familiar diminished seventh.

Diminished sevenths in various forms.

The diminished seventh is made up entirely of minor thirds piled up and is completely symmetrical; all of its so-called inversions have exactly the same sound as the original form.

If we start our seventh chord with a major third, we find two new kinds of seventh chords. The first is like a dominant seventh with a lowered fifth: also notated as 7–5.

This chord has two interlocking tritones, and the building blocks are major thirds surrounding a major second or major seconds surrounding a major third.

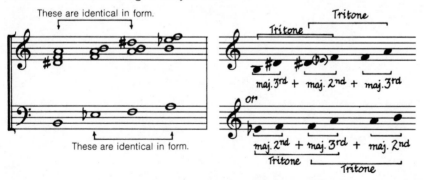

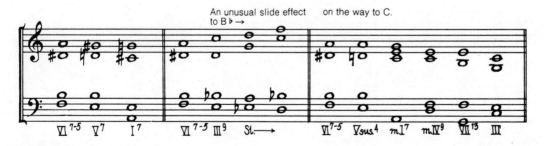

182

If we pile up two major thirds with a major second at either end or two major seconds with a major third at either end, we get still another form of seventh.

(II) 7+5 in various inversions.

This is like a dominant seventh with the fifth raised a half-step and is usually called 7+5.

7+5 chords used as secondary dominants or as slides.

$$V^{7+5} \quad I^9 \quad IV^{7+5} \quad VII^9 \quad V^{7+5} \quad Sl. \rightarrow IV^{7+5} \quad Sl. \rightarrow \quad V^{7+5} \quad I^9 \quad IV^{7+5} \quad VII^9$$

This chord has the form of and is often used as a dominant minor thirteenth (without a fifth, ninth, or eleventh).

We will talk more about this chord as a kind of dominant seventh in Building On Dominant Sevenths In Minor, page 185.

Here, in brief, are the four basic forms of these sevenths on a common bass.

As long as a chord has a "root" or keynote that you can hear and identify, we can say that we invert the chord by keeping the same notes (the same content) and putting one of the other notes in the bass. But when we are dealing with chords that have no real root-sense and which depend on context for their meaning, putting a different note into the bass very often changes the sound of the chord so radically that it can hardly be identified with its inversion. Most of the time, the uses of complex chords are linked to the note that actually occurs in the bass. When we build different versions of these chords on the same bass we get different content (different notes).

Keeping the bass.

Adjusting the bass to keep the same position.

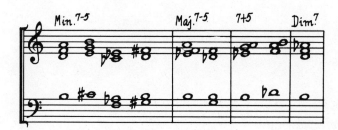

184

Building On Dominant Sevenths In Minor

You can build on seventh chords in the minor (just as we did in the major), and some new chord structures turn up.

Extensions of V⁷.

You can dispose of these 3.

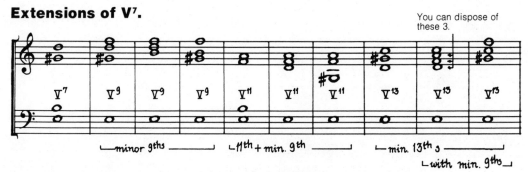

V^7 V^9 V^9 V^9 V^{11} V^{11} V^{11} V^{13} V^{13} V^{13}

└─minor 9ths─┘ └11th + min. 9th┘ └─min. 13ths─┘
                                                      └with min. 9ths┘

These are the forms that appear on the dominant seventh when you add the natural ninths, tenths, and thirteenths.

The major ninth on V^7 (F♯ over E^7) is used in minor as well as major. You can build minor thirteenths on this dominant major ninth like this.

Out of this . . . you can get this . . . or these.

└These are the most used.─┘

As we have seen, dominant minor thirteenths are often also notated as augmented fifths (7+5).

A note for guitarists: Neither of these notations (D^{13} or D^{7+5}) tells you what kind of ninth to play or which of a possible seven notes to omit. Guitar chords can be misleading; in much music with complex chords, guitarists are sometimes only given part of the chord to play. This has nothing to do with the playability of the chords; what happens is that the system of naming chords breaks down!

Here are some standard uses of V–I progressions using minor ninths and thirteenths in various forms.

inv. 13   inv. 13   inv. 9

These forms are even more useful on all the other degrees
where dominant sevenths occur.

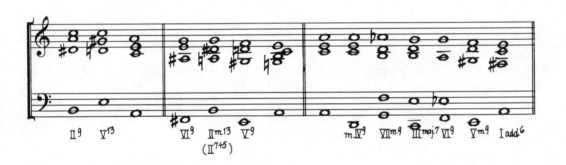

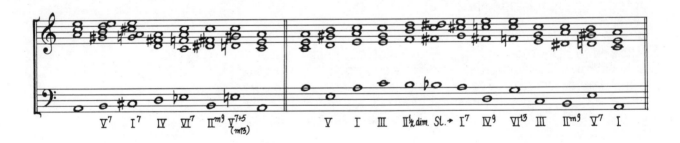

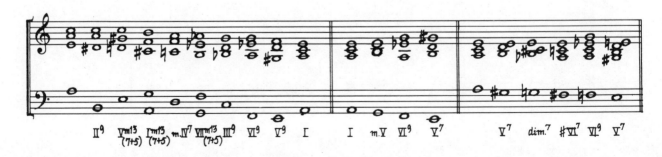

Diatonic Sevenths In Minor

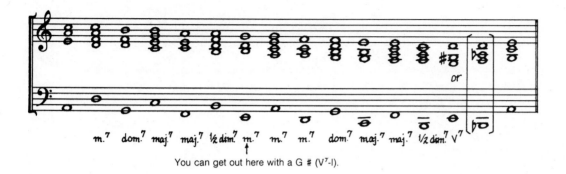

m.⁷ dom.⁷ maj.⁷ maj.⁷ ½ dim.⁷ m.⁷ m.⁷ m.⁷ dom.⁷ maj.⁷ maj.⁷ ½ dim.⁷ V⁷

or

You can get out here with a G # (V⁷-I).

The circle of diatonic sevenths in minor is less tonally clear than the corresponding circle of major sevenths. We've shown two octaves' worth, before making a clear A-minor cadence (with V⁷ or a slide chord).

The above cycle is based on the Aeolian form of the minor: here is the similar cycle using the Dorian minor (with the raised sixth degree).

m.I IV⁷ VII maj.⁷ III maj.⁷ #VI m.II⁷ m.V⁷ m.I⁷ IV⁷ VII maj.⁷ III maj.⁷ m#VI⁷ II⁷ V⁷
                        ½ dim.

The two modes can be mixed.

m.IV VII⁷ III maj.⁷ #VI m.II⁷ V⁷ I   I   IV⁷ VII maj.⁷ III maj.⁷ #VI II⁷ V⁷
                       ½ dim.   ½ dim.

Another version with inversions.

Chaining with mixed sevenths and ninths.

These are the principal sevenths and ninths on the various steps of the minor scale.

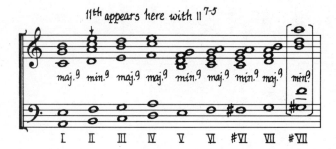

Some elaborations of a basic progression (I–IV–V–I).

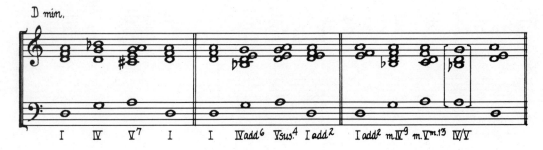

Modal minor picks up natural sevenths and other added-tone
chords very easily.

m.I⁷ VIIadd⁶ I⁷ V⁷ IV⁷ m.I⁷ VIIadd⁶ III V⁷ III I⁷ m.IV⁹ VII⁹sus.4

Mixing modal and tonal minor.

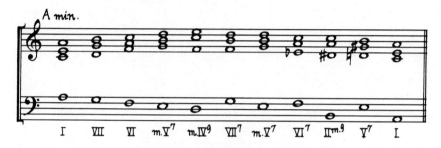

A min.

I VII VI m.V⁷ m.IV⁹ VII⁷ m.V⁷ VI⁷ IIm.⁹ V⁷ I

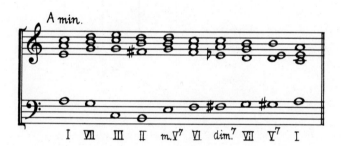

A min.

I VII III II m.V⁷ VI dim.⁷ VII V⁷ I

D min.

I IVadd² I IVadd² m.I⁷ III VII mV II I
                                    (VII)

A min.

III⁷ VImaj⁷ #VI½dim. II¹¹ V

Song skeletons.

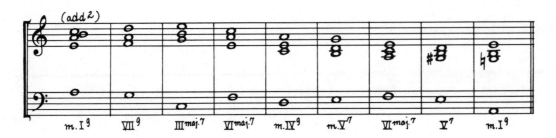

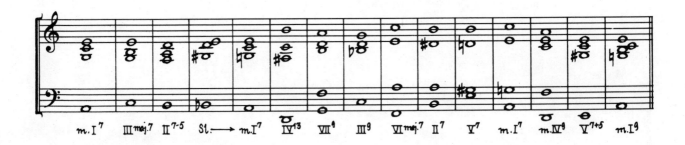

Substituting over a bass.

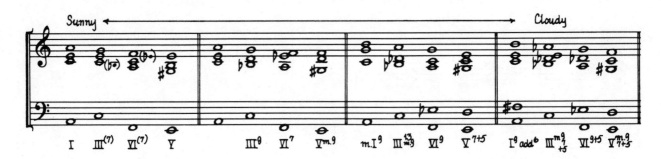

Slide Chords In The Minor

Slide chords are particularly important in minor progressions. As we have seen, two of the diatonic triads in minor easily lend themselves to acting as slide chords.

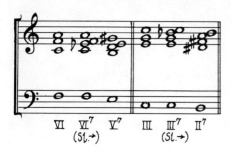

As we have already seen, any dominant seventh can function either as a secondary dominant or as a slide chord, and slide chords can be substituted more or less at any point in a secondary dominant chain.

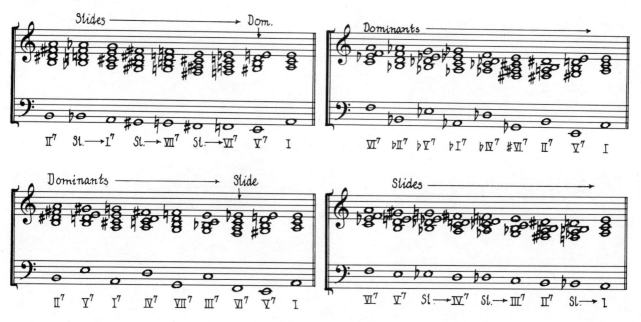

Here is a similar sequence with the 7–5 form of the slide chord alternating with secondary dominants.

If we use the bottom line as the bass, we see and hear very clearly how each secondary dominant "resolves" to a 7–5 instead of to a triad, or, as in the previous chain, to another secondary dominant. But if we omit the bottom line and let the bottom note in the right hand serve as the bass, we see and hear how the 7–5 slides down to the next dominant seventh in the chain.

191

Here is the same sequence with the order exchanged; that is, the first chord is a 7–5, the second a dominant seventh, and so on.

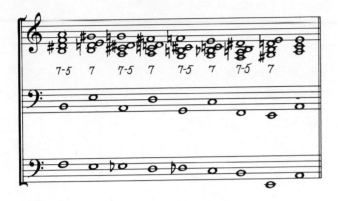

Here is the same sequence with half-diminished chords alternating with dominant sevenths.

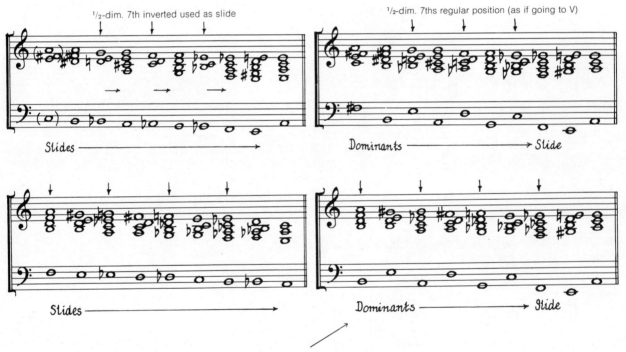

The half-diminished seventh form on this side acts like a II⁷ going to a V⁷; any of these diminished sevenths may, therefore, be used to prepare any secondary dominant.

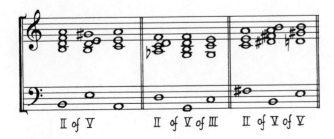

More Added-note Chords

Any of the chords that "prepare" a dominant seventh may have ninths, elevenths, or thirteenths piled on. Note that the more elaborate the preparatory chord, the more likely that the chords that follow will also be added-note chords.

Substitutions for secondary dominants.

Since slide chords are also approach chords, they can also have a superstructure of ninths, elevenths, and thirteenths.

Substitutions for slides.

Here is a real-life sequence of slides using these elements as they are used in typical pop sequences of the Thirties.

Each slide is different, instead of a mechanical sequence, as in the chords.

More On Preparing V

Any secondary dominant—V or V⁷ of X—can be prepared in three ways:

   V of V of X
   II of X
   slide of V of X

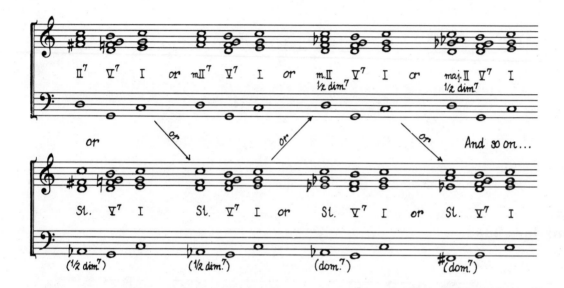

Remember that what is shown here for sevenths applies to forms using ninths, elevenths, and thirteenths, as can be seen (heard) in the next examples.

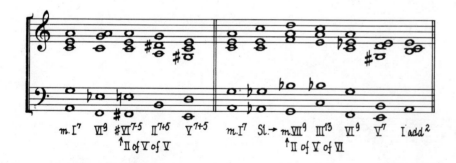

We are getting to the outer reaches of that planetary system we call tonality: being in a key. Ninth, eleventh, and thirteenth chords—especially in inversions and with the various alterations—are structures capable of sending us right out of the key, even into atonality.

In classical music, this kind of usage led to atonality.

A great deal of music from the Thirties to the present day preserves the sense of key, even though it makes extensive use of these chords. As the clarity and directional power of the tritone in the dominant seventh is obscured, this chord no longer defines the key by itself. However, regularity of rhythm and phrase, the places where the melody goes and the limitations on where the bass can go, all work together to keep the center intact. Only in free jazz are these elements opened up, "releasing" the chords, but that is beyond the scope of this book.

Chains Of Sevenths, Ninths, And Thirteenths

The principle of the interchangeability of secondary dominants and slides—with all the various seventh, ninth, eleventh, and thirteenth forms—creates slide chains which are found everywhere from big-band writing to Muzak to pop arranging to advanced composition. The trick in using them is figuring out where to get on and where to get off.

The secondary dominant and the slide chord that substitutes for it are always a tritone apart.

Slide chains with dominant ninths and dominant thirteenths.

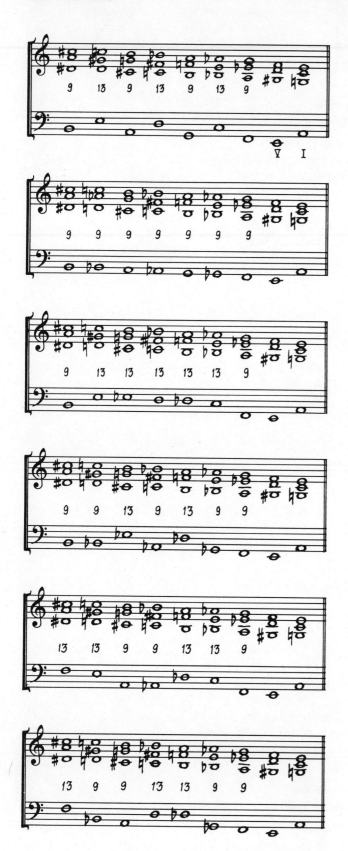

Slide chords with dominant ninths and dominant sevenths.

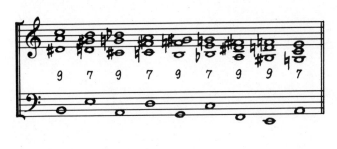

Minor and major half-diminished seventh slide/chains.

Dominants on this side.

Slides on this side.

I thought I heard Buddy Bolden say,
"You're terrible, you're awful, take it away."
S. Bechet

Major And Minor

We treat major and minor as separate topics for convenience and because of the tradition of European classical harmony. However, in vernacular harmony, there is a multiplicity of modal inputs and, in fact, major and minor are really the two poles of a continuum.

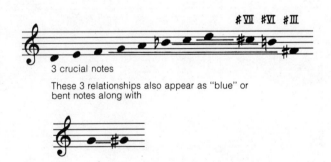

Blue or bent notes, African in origin, are melodic forms typically used with tonal harmony at the interface between modes.

Major-Minor Borrowings

Chords that arise in the major can be used in the minor and vice versa.

Certain chords with which we are already familiar—♭VII, ♭III, ♭VI, and even IV⁷—can be looked upon as modal borrowings of one sort or another, particularly with added sevenths, ninths, etc.

TTLT Beatles: "For No One"

Some standard progressions using modal mixtures (borrowings).

Many recent modal songs move quite freely in the "super-key." Such progressions often move from the simple triads to more complex chords.

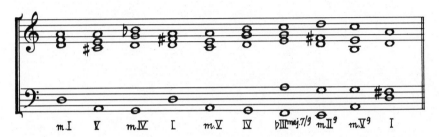

Minor V.

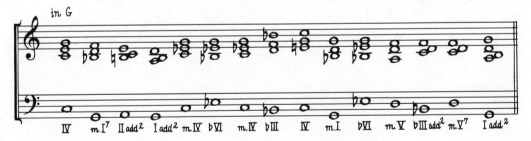

Using half-diminished sevenths as a form of I⁷, borrowed from the minor, in secondary dominant sequences.

Some song backgrounds using modal borrowings.

Lewis, Hamilton: "How High the Moon"

Teddy Randazzo, Bobby Weinstein: "(I Think I'm) Goin' Out of My Head"

Joni Mitchell: "Michael from Mountains"

Complex chords found in the minor—ninths, elevenths, and thirteenths of various kinds built on dominant and non-dominant sevenths—can of course be used in major keys as well.

The same with a few slide chords, instead of secondary dominants.

Although there are many tunes and progressions that use modal borrowings in connection with triads and seventh chords, the free harmonic mixing of modes is common in progressions using complex chords.

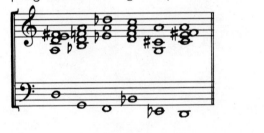 

We have not given the chord names in these examples. Can you identify them?

TTLT Beatles: "Taxman"
Jimi Hendrix: "Purple Haze"
Grateful Dead: "Till the Morning Comes" (chorus)
Grateful Dead: "Black Peter"

Mixture Chords

In effect, the mixture of major and minor modes creates a kind of super key, out of which a tremendous variety of harmonic resources can be drawn without weakening the key feeling. One of the characteristic chords of this mixture is a seventh that is both major and minor. This usually takes the form of a dominant seventh below, with the minor effect on top.

This chord is typically used on I, IV, V, and II.

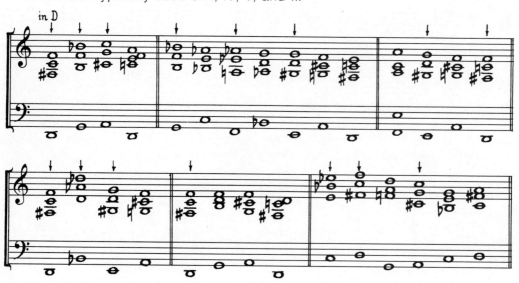

Mixture chords and minor thirteenth (7+5) chords are found together.

Other Mixtures

In the same way that you can mix a major and a minor third, you
can also mix two forms of other intervals.

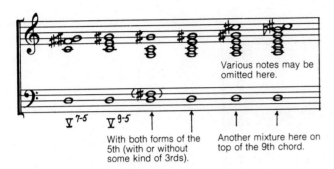

Various notes may be
omitted here.

$\underline{V}^{7-5}$ $\underline{V}^{9-5}$

With both forms of the
5th (with or without
some kind of 3rds).

Another mixture here on
top of the 9th chord.

Two different fifths:

Adding a note to the diminished seventh.

Substitutions Harmonizing Melodic Formulas

Mixtures and borrowings create a great number of options. In these examples, we take a melodic formula and give as many harmonic variations as we can think of.

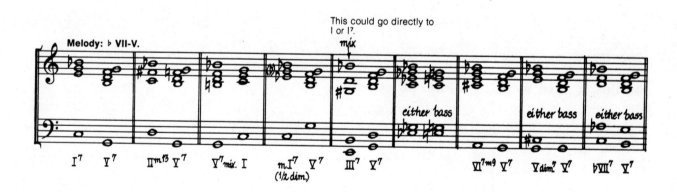

207

Altered Degrees And Their Chords

In the four basic modes that we have been using, only the C mode has the leading tone or semi-tone below the tonic.

Because of the special push to the tonic, this leading tone effect is often borrowed for use in the other modes and has been a normal use in those modes alongside the flat seventh for literally centuries.

In the same way, the fourth degree comes to be raised up in tonal harmony in order to create a push to V—as in the secondary dominant to V.

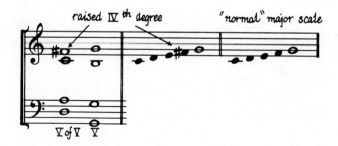

Closer to our own time, the lowered second degree provides another push to I.

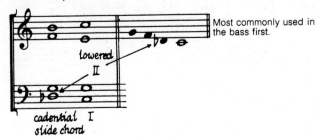

Most commonly used in the bass first.

As a result of the growing familiarity with these auxiliary scale degrees, the chords on these degrees become incorporated into the harmonic language quite as freely as chords built on the original modal degrees.

The raised seventh degree has a natural diminished triad in both major and minor which, as we have seen, is occasionally used.

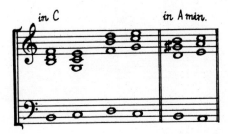

More common is the diminished seventh on the same degree.

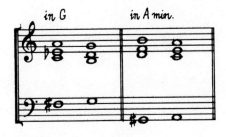

The half-diminished chord on the leading tone can work the same way.

But in major, at least, it usually works in the secondary dominant chain going to III or III[7] on the way to VI.

This chord is important because, in one form or another, it is used to establish VI, the relative minor.

Other sevenths on the leading tone.

Lennon-McCartney use this in several songs.

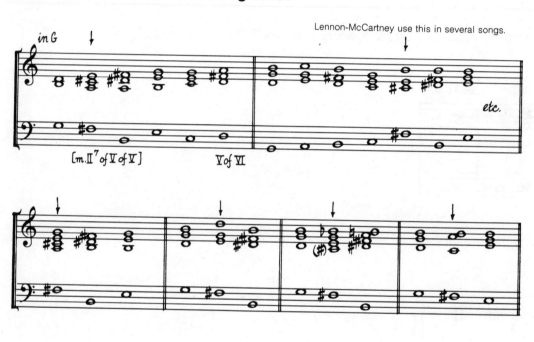

TTLT Beatles: "Here, There and Everywhere"

Or it can simply be part of a standard secondary dominant chain.

210

A plain major or minor triad on #VII is occasionally used, but #VII⁷ going to III or sometimes back to I is sometimes used.

There is a parallel series of chords available on the raised fourth degree—C# in G—which can go to #VII⁷ in a secondary dominant sequence.

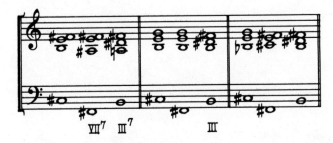

However, the usual meaning of the raised fourth degree is quite different. It generally arises as a passing chord on the way to some form of V or I$^6_4$.

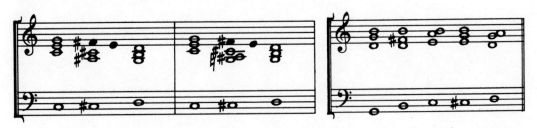

A few more forms on #IV.

diminished 7th s

Going to V via II.

IV⁷ as V of VII.

#IV is not to be confused with a ♭V, a chord which occasionally appears in passages like this.

II⁷ ♭V⁷ IV⁷ I
    SL.→

Sliding through flat areas using the chain on ♮ II.

Chords built on the lowered second degrees are mostly used in final cadences as slide chords to I.

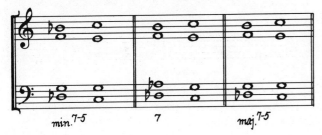

The classical formula is not much used.

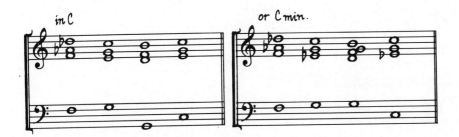

The dominant seventh chord on the flat second degree (or the raised tonic) can be used as part of the circle of secondary dominants.

♭II can be reached by using a secondary dominant on ♭VI.

Lennon and McCartney use the ambiguous diminished seventh on ♭II as a slide chord—the first time back to I, the second time to go to IV.

Lennon-McCartney: "Because"

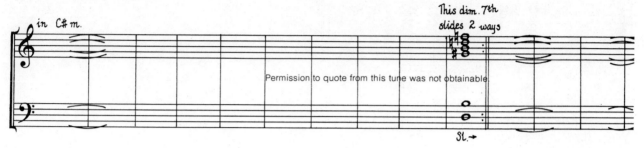

Going round on the flat side.

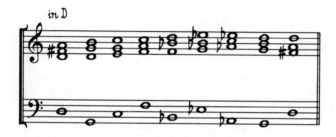

Here is a ninth chord on the flat second degree going to V¹³.

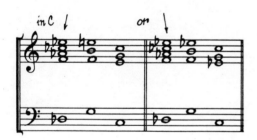

A common form with F in the bass.

The second sequence uses a half-diminished seventh on F, a closely related chord.

Here is D♭–C used, not in a cadence, but as part of a progression.

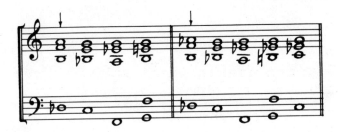

Minor triads, seventh and ninth chords on ♭II, are also possible in both major and minor keys.

This Lennon-McCartney progression has the following features:

Major-minor borrowings.
Secondary dominants.
Minor V⁷.
Chord on II as slide to I.

Lennon-McCartney: "Things We Said Today"

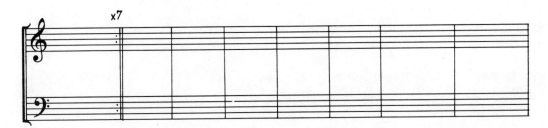

Permission to quote from this tune was not obtainable.

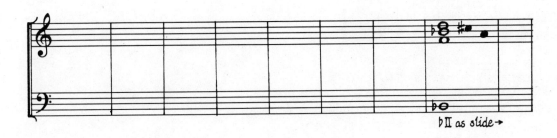

♭II as slide→

215

More On Key

Most vernacular harmony defines a stable harmonic area and stays there. I^7—the dominant seventh form—is a common keynote chord in the blues. Any of the following chords can represent I in the key of G.

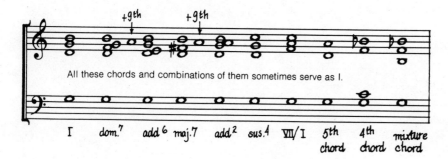

All these chords and combinations of them sometimes serve as I.

It isn't necessary to start out on I. Here are the changes for "Salty Dog," a prototypical walkaround used in hundreds of songs.

The trick is to start somewhere in the middle of a progression, creating a moment of weightlessness. Of course, as soon as you move one step along, you know where you are.

Green, Heyman, Sour, Eyton: "Body and Soul"

As we have already seen and heard, it is possible to go very far out harmonically without losing the sense of key if there is some kind of tonal payoff at the polar places in the phrase. From another point of view, the fact that even the far-out chords move in a tonal way or are constantly being measured against a basic key gives these chords a certain feeling, clarity, and comprehensibility.

"When I Was Out in the Cold" from *Stauf*

Michael Sahl and Eric Salzman

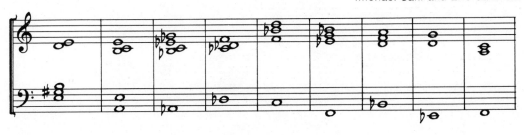

Going round between minor and major.

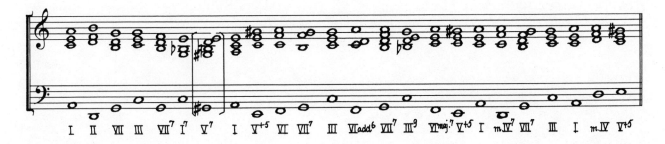

Hovering between relative major and minor keys is a common way to expand the sense of key.

Janis Ian: "Society's Child"

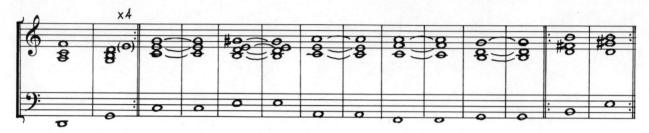

Instead of being restricted by a chain or pattern, it is possible to borrow chords from both sides of the relative major-minor seesaw.

Lennon-McCartney: "Michelle"

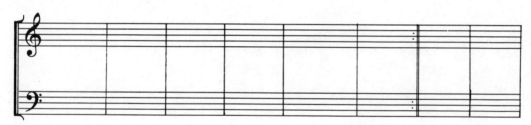

Permission to quote from this tune was not obtainable.

TTLT Paul Simon: "El Condor Pasa (If I Could)"
                    "Duncan"
                    "At the Zoo"

A modal harmony with sevenths increases the sense of ambiguity.

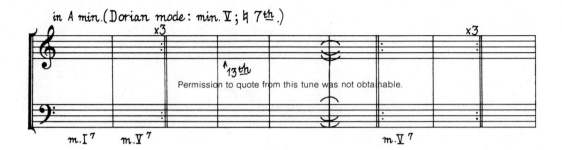

Added-note chords—diatonic sevenths, ninths, added sixths, and so forth—increase the ambiguity between relative major and minor.

So far, we have treated the music in this book as if it didn't change key. In fact, there is a large gray area between movement through closely related harmonic areas and full-scale key changes or modulations.

Typically, a new harmonic area is introduced in the **bridge**. This may be a movement in the direction of a closely related key (the subdominant, the relative minor or major) or a strong new key area or an unstable (or "weird") bridge that wanders.

TTLT Beatles: "I Want to Hold Your Hand" (bridge in subdominant)
Fats Waller: "Ain't Misbehavin'" (bridge in relative minor)

Modulation or key wandering is not necessarily confined to the
bridge. Sometimes the main body of the song wanders too.

Jim Webb: "Up, Up and Away"

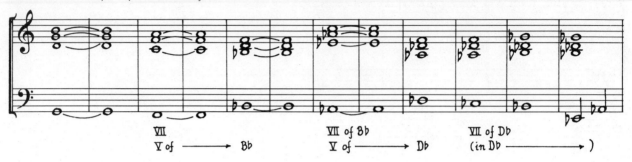

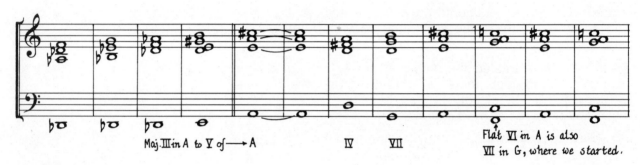

No matter how far out the bridge gets, the stable song form tells you that you are in the bridge and that you must go back.

THE GIRL FROM IPANEMA (GAROTA DE IPANEMA)

Music by ANTONIO CARLOS JOBIM
English Words by NORMAN GIMBEL
Original Words by VINICIUS DE MORAES

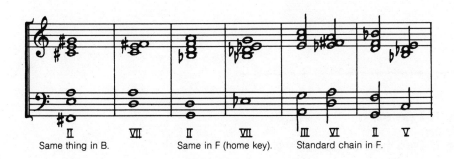

FINAL WARNING

At this point we are not talking just about harmony, but about composition.

Chord changes don't exist in themselves. They come out of and create phrases. Every aspect of harmony, from simple changes to modulations, makes sense as part of phrase and phrase and structure—in other words, of music.

A chord is not a machine. All that we have done is narrow what we're looking at down to chords, chord structures, and changes, but that is not the secret of making music. The secret is no secret, but simply the total interaction of melody, bass, rhythm, phrase, and harmony.

Traveller: **Where do I get to if I go on up this road?**
Settler: **Don' know, don' know.**
Traveller: **Where do I get to if I go back the way I came?**
Settler: **Don' know, don' know.**
Traveller: **What is this place called?**
Settler: **Don' know, don' know.**
Traveller: **You don't know much, do you?**
Settler: **No, but I ain't lost.**

The Arkansas Traveller

About the Authors

Michael Sahl, born in Boston in 1934, is a composer of serious and popular music. He studied at Amherst, Princeton, and in Europe. He has served as music director of WBAI—a non-commercial, listener-supported FM station in New York—and has appeared as a pianist with the Center for Performing Arts at Buffalo, the East First Street Free Band, and the Free Music Store, and as organist at Spencer Memorial Church. He has played classical music, avant-garde music, jazz, ragtime, folk rock, gospel, and his own work, which is of an eclectic character. In 1968–69 he toured as a pianist with Judy Collins and recorded *Who Knows Where the Time Goes* with her; she recorded his "Prothalamium" on her subsequent album, *Whales and Nightingales*. Other music has been recorded on Cardinal ("A Mitzvah for the Dead"), Lyrichord ("Tropes on the Salve Regina"), and Desto ("String Quartet 1969").

Eric Salzman, born in New York in 1933, studied at Columbia, Princeton, and in Europe. He has served as music director for WBAI—where he founded the Free Music Store—and has written for many publications here and abroad, including *The New York Times* and *The New York Herald-Tribune*; he is currently a contributing critic for *Stereo Review*. His textbook on twentieth-century music is the most widely used in the field. His works have been recorded on Nonesuch (*The Nude Paper Sermon*) and Atlantic-Finnadar (*Wiretap*, including "Larynx Music" and "Helix"). The Quog Music Theater/La Mama production of his *Lazarus* toured in Europe in 1975. Some of his other multi-media and music-theater works have been produced by and for public television in New York and Syracuse, the Perspective Encounters of Pierre Boulez and the New York Philharmonic, and the Roundhouse concerts of the BBC.

The musical collaborations by the authors of this book include *The Conjurer* (produced by Joseph Papp at the New York Shakespeare Festival's Public Theater in 1975) and *Stauf* (produced by Quog Music Theater at the Cubiculo in New York City in 1976).